CONTROVERSIES

Controversies was written specifically for use in RHE 306 classes at the University of Texas at Austin. The book teaches basic lessons in research, analysis, and argumentation to help students learn college-level writing and critical-thinking skills. Inside are exercises, assignment prompts, sample student works, and extended explanations of key concepts.

TABLE OF CONTENTS | # Controversies

| # What is a Controversy?

I t's the title of your textbook, and it's the subject of RHE 306. While taking this class, you will research, analyze, and contribute to one of these. So what is a "controversy"? Here's the simplest answer and the easiest way to think about the subject of RHE 306: A controversy is something people argue about in public. And if it were really that simple, then you could skip this introduction and jump right into your first major assignment. But, as you will learn over the course of Unit 1, a controversy can be very complicated. In fact, your job in the first unit of RHE 306 is to explain a recent public controversy to someone who doesn't know about it, to someone who may be interested, to someone who should know about it but doesn't understand why it is a controversy. We call this *mapping the controversy*—explaining the history and the present state of a debate to an interested but uninformed audience. Before you begin to research or write about a controversy, read this chapter to better understand what a controversy is and how to approach it. Let's start with an example.

Let's begin with a recent controversy: In the spring of 2015, the Texas legislature approved a bill that would allow concealed handguns on university campuses. The legislature also began to consider a second bill that would allow people with gun licenses to carry holstered guns openly. We live in a country where Second Amendment rights are broadly interpreted and rigorously enforced. We also live in a country where gun violence is common and tragic. So you won't be surprised to learn that these bills sparked heated argument. At a glance, you might conclude that the disagreement was between those who oppose gun safety and those who want a comfortable environment for learning. Or you might conclude that the controversy was between those who want to protect constitutional rights and those who want to take those rights away. But neither of these descriptions is fair to the people or their arguments. In fact, both of these characterizations present the controversy from very biased perspectives. In this chapter, and in the first unit of this course, we encourage you to take a careful and critical view of controversies: to understand what's really at stake; to fairly see the issue from several perspectives; and to effectively advocate your viewpoint.

Think about the concealed and open-carry bills in the Texas state legislature. Needless to say, many people wanted to protect Second Amendment rights. Such people typically get represented by professional political organizations (such as Open Carry

Texas). Such organizations may or may not be from the immediate community. Open Carry Tarrant County, for instance, has little to do with the University of Texas. This organization is not even connected to Travis County, where UT is located. Yet Open Carry Tarrant County supported the bill to allow concealed weapons on Texas college campuses because they have a broader mission. The larger organization (Open Carry Texas) boldly announces its purpose on their homepage (opencarrytexas.org): "We're dedicated to the safe and legal carry of firearms openly in the state of Texas." No mention of Travis county or UT. If gun-rights advocates are one group of stakeholders, university students are another. Some UT students, in the aftermath of shootings at other American universities, fear for their safety. Some want the right to carry a firearm, a right they exercise (safely) elsewhere. Furthermore, university personnel have a stake in this matter. Many professors may feel uncomfortable around firearms and prefer that their classrooms be a firearm free zone. Local police worry about safety but also cost. The chief of the Austin police, Art Acevedo, stated publicly that open carry legislation would require more extensive training for local police, training that would raise the cost of local law enforcement. And finally, the university administration had a stake in these bills. Universities must represent the interests of faculty, staff, and students. Since faculty and students often have conflicted opinions, the university chancellors have refused to take a firm stand. The Texas A&M System Chancellor, John Sharp, said that he wanted his students to enjoy the same rights and privileges both on and off campus. Sharp's statement implies but does not openly support the concealed or open-carry bills. The UT System Chancellor, Wiliam McRaven, stated that he was concerned about safety but more concerned about funding higher education. McRaven's statement, like Sharp's, attempts to capture the concerns of UT staff, students, and faculty without firmly condemning these bills. The basic idea here is that the controversy about concealed and open-carry legislation on Texas university campuses was complicated.

Brief Exercise: Controversies often focus on particular actions— legislative bills, city council ordinances, school board decisions. These are policies, plans for action, and they tend to be at the center of the most heated controversies. In your local communities, what policies are people arguing about? What policies are they debating? Who is interested in these debates and why? Are you interested in this debate? Should you be? Does the policy affect you or something you care about?

Like most real controversies, this one can't be reduced to simple "pro" and "con" or "point" and "counterpoint." When mapping such a controversy, you have to look for its complexity.

At the end of Unit 1, you will analyze a similar controversy. It doesn't have to be specific to UT, though your controversy may be local. It doesn't have to be about a piece of legislation. People argue about lots of things—what to do, what to care about, what to believe. Your controversy may be national in scope: Should people in the United States believe that global warming is caused by human activity? Your controversy may focus on a particular state: Should Texas expand Medicaid to cover more people? Your controversy may be international: Should Western nations offer military support to rebels in Syria?

In our introductory example, we focus on a controversy that is particular to the state of Texas. But some controversies apply to states and to the entire country. For instance, the University of Texas considers students' race in the admissions process, in an effort at increasing the diversity of its student body. Such a "race-conscious" admissions policy is very specific to UT. However, if this admissions policy turns out to be unconstitutional, as alleged in a Supreme Court case (*Fisher v. University of Texas*), then the controversy will be national because many universities in the country have similarly race-conscious admissions policies. And controversies can change as well. If the Supreme Court decides in favor of Abigail Fisher, then the University of Texas will have to rethink its efforts at increasing diversity through admissions policies. And there will surely be debate about the new policies. Similarly, after the Texas legislature passed both the concealed and the open carry bills, there was much debate about what policies and procedures UT would have to put in place. The question stopped being, "Should we allow concealed weapons on campus?" The bill signed into Texas law allows the particular universities to determine "safe zones" where guns are not allowed. As a result, after the summer of 2015, the question became, "In what specific areas should we not allow concealed weapons on campus?" Furthermore, the debate about concealed weapons on college campus is moving outside of the state of Texas to other places, where state legislatures are considering laws that allow concealed carry on their own campuses.

Whatever it is, your controversy must have certain qualities. It must be *public*. It must be *recent*. It must have *stakeholders*. And it must include a range of *viewpoints*. Since these terms—*public, recent, stakeholders*, and *viewpoints*—are so important, you should consider each in greater detail. This vocabulary will become the foundation for your future research and writing. Knowing these terms and their definitions will help you to choose a controversy that you can map.

Public Controversies

People argue constantly—about clothing styles, movie preferences, religious beliefs, state laws, and workplace habits. We tend to think of these controversies as either *public* or *private*. A *private* controversy affects only those in a particular relationship, organization, or company. You can disagree with your roommates about the merits of a musical genre. "Dubstep is the greatest thing since reggae." "Reggae is boring, and dubstep is worse." But the controversy remains *private* because your personal musical preferences will not affect many people. It won't even affect your roommate if you always wear headphones. However, whether or not you get to play your music loudly late at night is a *public* matter because the noise will affect everyone in your neighborhood or building. A company can require its employees to wear suits and skirts below the knee. Again, the matter is private because it will not affect anyone outside that corporate culture. A fraternity can require pledges to endure humiliating rituals. And, as long as those rituals don't endanger anyone's health or make anyone liable for another person's injury, hazing remains a private matter.

Public controversies arise when some people want to do something that will affect many others—people outside a given club, company, or social network. It's hard to separate *public* from *private* controversies. Some people argue that music preference becomes a public issue when certain genres of music promote violent or reckless behaviors. Some people argue that corporate culture becomes a public issue when certain habits lead to discrimination. Strict dress codes may make the workplace hostile to or uncomfortable for particular groups. If some people are not given an equal opportunity to succeed, then a strict dress code has notable public consequences. Finally, some people argue that fraternity hazing becomes a public issue when pledges get injured or when they die. Friends and families—the university community—suffer.

Here are a few qualities that should help you to identify *public* controversies.

First, many people from different perspectives are debating the matter. When lots of people who have different interests care about the issue, then typically the controversy affects enough people to be a *public* matter.

Second, people are debating the issue in public spaces. This second criterion raises an immediate question: What's a public space? If we lived hundreds of years ago, then

Brief Exercise: Identify a website as *public* or *private*. Go to tumblr.com, pinterest. com, or wordpress.com. Browse a few blogs/pages/pins. (You will have to create accounts with Wordpress and Pinterest to browse their selection of pages and pins, but many Tumblr sites will be available without signing in.) In order to decide if this is a public or private site, ask yourself the following questions:

- Does this site feature opinions and beliefs about matters that will likely affect many different people or even everyone in a society?
- Does this venue address an audience with various interests and beliefs—not just people who belong to a particular club, work for a particular company, or share an appreciation for a certain kind of art or music?
- Is this venue available to all or most of the people in a community or society?

Present evidence to support your claim that this is a public or private venue. For example, you might say, "This website is mostly a private venue because it features articles about the best fabrics for making quilts, and quilt-making is unlikely to affect anyone other than quiltmakers and fabric manufacturers. Furthermore, the website is hosted by the *Quiltmaker's Club*, a magazine that sells patterns to hobbyists. Only people with a particular interest are likely to read the magazine or consult the website. Finally, the comments about the articles are written by quiltmakers."

the "public" space would literally be a space, an open area in the center of a town or a city where people gathered to discuss, to hear speeches, and to make decisions. Town squares and plazas are examples of such public spaces. Today, however, no one goes to the local park, stands on a soap box, and orates about the need for ground troops in the Middle East, the problem with farm subsidies, or the decay of American culture. Nowadays, people debate public issues in various *media* and various *venues*. The *media* include print, the Internet, and television. (There are other media, of course: street theater, graffiti, music.) The *venues* include newspapers, books, magazines, websites, and television programs. The involvement of such media and venues doesn't provide surefire proof that a controversy is public. People discuss plenty of private matters on blogs and on the comments threads of various websites. Lots of television is about private matters—what to wear, how to plan a wedding, what's (not) funny. And many newspapers and magazines focus on shopping and tabloid journalism, decidedly private matters. You're looking for mostly *public* venues: the opinion/editorial pages of any newspaper; television programs featuring debate or one strong viewpoint; websites focused on commentary rather than news reporting.

Third, when expressing their interests, values, and beliefs, people try to persuade others who may not share their interests, values, and beliefs. Of course, in many private controversies, we try to appeal to our audiences. However, in private matters it is always

Further Discussion: Why is it so difficult to identify the *venues* of public argument nowadays? Why can't we just go to one place where everyone gathers to talk about public affairs? Such a single place existed and was used a long time ago. The Roman *forum* was a large space in the middle of a city, a place where people shopped. Since everyone came there regularly, public officials (senators, consuls, and so forth) often spoke publicly about the affairs of the state. They stood at a *rostrum* and orated about the *res publicae*, the public affairs. Sometimes an orator would simply stand and deliver news about an ongoing war or a recent law. Sometimes an orator would try to drum up support for a military campaign or a proposed law. In modern society, after the printing press was invented and literacy became more widespread, newspapers and pamphlets took the forum's place. As recently as the eighteenth century, when there were many who could not read, people still gathered in the town square (also a common location for the market) to hear someone read the newspaper aloud. Reading newspapers aloud to illiterate citizens also occurred in public houses (bars) and coffeehouses where they spent their leisure time, and in factories where they worked. Nowadays, most people can read, so print culture has all but replaced oral delivery. In this brief historical narrative, you can see a major shift in public media and venue. From oral media to print. From the venue of the forum to that of the newspaper. Can we call the move from newspapers to the Internet another major shift? Is Twitter replacing the *New York Times* just as the *New York Times* replaced the town square? In what other *media* and *venues* do we now discuss *public* affairs?

easier to "preach to the choir," that is, to tell the audience things they already agree with or believe, because people who belong to the same club or work for the same corporation likely have similar beliefs and interests. Public controversies, on the other hand, affect and attract people with a broad range of interests, values, and beliefs. So, in order to be widely persuasive, people arguing in public controversies must address many different interests. You might notice that people use a few common argumentative moves in public controversies when they are trying to persuade others who don't share their interests, values, or beliefs. Speakers might directly address specific audience members. They might concede that what specific audience members believe is true. They might refute beliefs held by specific audience members.

Brief Exercise: A number of online news sites collect articles from a variety of sources. The Yahoo News site (news.yahoo.com) collects articles from other news outlets. Reddit.com also collects articles (and other media) on a number of topics. Visit one of these "news aggregator" sites, or use your own (such as Google News). Find an article that interests you. Is this article addressed to a public or a private audience? To answer this question, look for the following features, which are typical to public arguments:

- *Direct Address to Specific Audience Members*: The speaker identifies and tries to speak to a particular group of people. For example: "Some conservatives worry about divorce rates. Many conservatives believe that we should do everything we can to keep families together. To them I say, you're right. And the best way to keep families together is to keep them financially stable. That's why extending unemployment benefits is the right thing to do. A family with unemployed parents is more likely to shatter under the stress of financial hardship."
- *Concession*: The speaker admits something the audience believes to be true. For example: "Some liberals believe that the government should not tell us who we can love. And I agree that the government should be kept out of our bedrooms and out of our hearts. But adoption is not just about love. It's about parenthood and families. When we have adoption laws that favor married couples, we're not telling people that they cannot love one another. We're telling people that we want our children to grow up in stable families where they are likely to prosper."
- *Refutation*: The speaker fairly represents an opponent's viewpoint and then tries to explain why the opponent is mistaken. For example: "Environmentalists worry that hydrofracking will result in polluted water supplies. This can happen if we are not careful. But technological developments and strict regulations have all but removed the threat of water pollution due to hydrofracking."

Copy and paste (or transcribe) the segment that you think is a refutation, concession, or a direct address to a specific type of audience member. Explain why you think this section demonstrates the speaker is trying to appeal to people who might not share the speaker's interests, values, or beliefs.

Recent Controversies

Right now, no one in the United States is debating whether slavery should be legal. No one is debating whether the United States should be part of Great Britain. And no one is debating whether the Taliban should govern Afghanistan. All three of these controversies are past. And all three were resolved by force. People are debating controversies that can still be resolved with words. They care about *recent* controversies.

Look for something that people are debating right now, some question that people seem able or willing to resolve without protests, violence, or threats. We suggest that

Further Discussion: A few years ago, someone scrawled the following graffiti (also pictured below) in an effort to make an argument: "Fiat Currency Doesn't Work." Someone else, as you can see, responded by crossing out "Fiat Currency" and writing "Gold Standard."

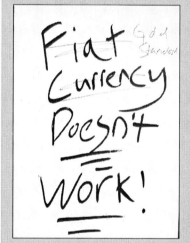
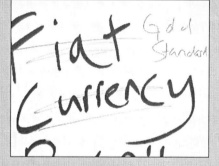

Do these two arguments engage a larger controversy? It's hard for us to figure out what they are arguing about. And this is why mapping a controversy is so important. These two people are arguing about whether the United States government should keep and exchange gold for paper money. Such a "gold standard," some claim, reduces inflation. "Fiat currency" is money whose value depends not on any promise of gold but on the government's authority (a "fiat"). Believe it or not, you are looking at one moment in an *ongoing* controversy about how to ensure the value of U.S. currency—by gold or fiat—a controversy that goes back more than a century. For most of its history, the U.S. promised some gold in exchange for (some of) its paper money. The gold standard for U.S. dollars steadily weakened over the twentieth century and was eventually removed completely in 1973. Some people still want to bring it back. Is this a *recent* controversy? Can you think of another controversy that requires this kind of "mapping" (history, explanation of participants, summary of arguments) in order to understand what's being debated and why?

there is a critical time—after people are affected and before they are fed up—when they can resolve their differences with arguments. You are looking for a controversy with argumentative possibility.

A *past* controversy has already been resolved. People no longer argue about whether the United States should have a public retirement system because we agreed to create Social Security. Now, however, we argue about how much the public retirement system should provide for each citizen. People no longer argue about how we should deal with the AIDS epidemic in the United States because anti-retroviral drugs have largely made AIDS a chronic condition, something manageable with proper medical treatment. Now we argue about how to make such anti-retroviral drugs more widely available and how to prevent the further spread of HIV.

An *ongoing* controversy flares up and goes away as circumstances inspire people to revisit old disagreements. In the United States, citizens have entertained ongoing controversies about race relations, income inequality, gender equality, and social customs, to name just a few. Throughout the nineteenth and twentieth centuries, for instance, people debated the "proper" economic roles in a heterosexual marriage. At first, people debated whether a woman could own property. Then people debated whether a woman could or should work outside the home. And then they debated whether a woman should have a career with equal pay. (Many still debate the question of equal pay.) Now we debate whether a man should be guaranteed family leave from work (paternity leave) equal to what's typically given a woman (maternity leave).

Ongoing controversies are gripping because they get at the longstanding divisions, the real disagreements, the big issues in a society. But they are also difficult to engage. You have to wait until the *ongoing* controversy becomes a *recent* controversy. Not everyone wants to talk about income or gender inequality all the time. We tend to revisit these debates when circumstances call us back. For example, in 1998 Lilly Ledbetter sued the General Motors Corporation for not paying her the same wage earned by men with similar status. She lost the case on technical grounds. Her loss in court prompted the U.S. Congress to pass the Lilly Ledbetter Fair Pay Act of 2009, which, in effect, removed the technicality that led the Supreme Court to rule against her. During the decade between Ledbetter's initial suit and the Ledbetter Act's approval, people revisited the issue of gender inequality in the workplace. Because of a Supreme Court case and a pending U.S. bill, an *ongoing* controversy became a *recent* controversy.

And that's what you're looking for—a recent controversy. You need not find a recent controversy that is part of an ongoing controversy. You may come upon something completely new, something no one has argued about before. At the moment, for example, people are debating how to regulate marijuana sales—something never before debated because no state had ever legalized marijuana until now. This is, in many ways,

Further Discussion: Controversies about race and criminal justice have been ongoing in the United States for many years. We have periodically debated several questions: Should police be allowed to use tactics—like stopping and frisking people at will—even when those tactics disproportionally affect people of color? Why are there so many people of color incarcerated? Recently, two kinds of events have made these ongoing controversies into recent controversies: police killing of innocent black men (or children) and protests against police treatment of certain populations. Which of these two events is more important? Did recent police actions cause an ongoing controversy about race and criminal justice to become recent? Or did the protests raise awareness about longstanding police behaviors? Or is there something else to consider? Can we attribute this recent controversy to the videos of particular police injuring people or the media's coverage of the court cases and protests? Many people attribute the 1960s controversies about civil rights to the media's use of video cameras. When Americans saw segregation and police violence against peaceful marchers on their television screens, they became interested. Can we say the same about the events in Ferguson, New York City, or Madison, Wisconsin? Did people finally start to care about race and criminal justice when they saw YouTube videos of Staten Island police choking a man or when they saw a cellphone video of a South Carolina officer shooting someone in the back?

a new controversy. It is related to an ongoing controversy about the public impact of marijuana use. In that regard, because certain states have legalized marijuana for recreational consumption, we have two controversies, both recent:

- An ongoing controversy—made recent by new laws: Does the personal use of marijuana have mostly good or mostly bad public consequences?
- A new controversy—made possible by new laws: How should we regulate the sale, distribution, and personal use of marijuana?

We can anticipate another new controversy that may erupt:

- How and when should we punish those caught driving while under the influence of marijuana?

Of course, this last question remains a *future* controversy, something we don't argue about (yet) because we do not yet feel or acknowledge the public effects of people smoking marijuana and driving. Once we do feel or acknowledge these effects—once a stoned driver kills a child—we will begin to debate this question.

In sum, you are looking for a controversy that elicits strong feelings, something people are debating right now because of some contemporary development. You want a *recent* controversy, not just an ongoing controversy and certainly not a past or a future controversy.

Brief Exercise: Pick up a newspaper (or go to a newspaper's website). Randomly select two opinion articles. After reading both, answer the following questions:
   • What controversy (major question) does each article try to address?
   • Is the controversy recent, past, or future?
      ○ If the opinion article addresses a recent controversy, what event prompted this debate?
      ○ If the opinion article addresses a past controversy, has the question already been settled, or is it ongoing?
      ○ If the article addresses a future controversy, what would have to happen for people to really start debating this question?
   • Based on your answers to the above questions, decide which article addresses a controversy that deserves to be mapped and explain why.

Stakeholders in a Controversy

So far, we have explained the status of a controversy by talking about its currency. A more current or recent controversy is likely to have higher status because we tend to care more about things that affect us now. We also care most about things that affect us most directly. People become *stakeholders* in a controversy when they feel they are or will be so affected that they must become directly involved. The stakeholders in any controversy are the ones most likely to write opinion columns, to collect signatures, to donate money, and to organize protests. The rest of us—those in the public who are indirectly affected by a controversy's outcome—tend to listen and vote, but we do not tend to get involved. Of course, a controversy with more stakeholders is likely to be more important. Consider the ongoing debate about the U.S. healthcare system. We are all stakeholders in this controversy because we all depend upon doctors, hospitals, and other medical services. As a result, this controversy will not go away anytime soon.

Knowing who the stakeholders are and why they care will help you understand why the controversy has taken a particular shape. In the current healthcare debate, for instance, you might wonder why people argue about whether all states must expand Medicaid. If we really want to give healthcare to everyone, then expanding coverage to include the poor sounds like a good idea, something we can all get behind. But to see why some people disagree, let's think about two groups of stakeholders: Some politicians have been elected to state office (state governors, senators, representatives). They have an interest—a stake—in maintaining local control over what their government does. A federal requirement (or incentive) to expand Medicaid takes some of that local control away. Other politicians, especially those elected to national office (the president, U.S. senators, and U.S. representatives) have a stake in expanding federal authority over state governments, especially when that authority allows them to do things they think right and good. So two stakeholders—local politicians and federal politicians—argue about expanding Medicaid. Federal politicians say the Medicaid expansion is a good extension of the federal government's authority. Local politicians say the Medicaid expansion is a bad infringement on state government. This example is, of course, oversimplified. Many members of the U.S. congress side with their state governments because they want to reduce the size of the federal government or for other reasons—the Medicaid expansion is costly, may be ineffective, and so forth. And many state officials favor the Medicaid expansion because they believe it will bring extra money to their local economies. Though oversimplified, this example is useful because it highlights two kinds of stakeholders and the reasons they have taken particular positions in this controversy. If you can similarly identify the stakeholders in your controversy, then you can begin to imagine what these people might say, based on their interests, their beliefs, and their values.

Before moving on to the next section, take a moment to think carefully about three terms we have used in this chapter so far and will use later in this textbook: *interest*, *belief*, and *value*. These three terms offer a useful way to analyze stakeholders.

Interests: These are the *stakes* in a controversy. People become interested typically because they are affected. Depending on the controversy's outcome, they stand to win or lose something. In the healthcare controversy mentioned above, politicians stand to win or lose authority. The healthcare controversy touches on many financial interests as well. Healthcare providers and medical-device manufacturers might gain or lose

Further Discussion: Interests and values can conflict, making some stakeholders uncomfortable. Consider the pro-choice bumper-sticker pictured here:

Without stating the point openly, this bumper-sticker asks us to think about the interest we have in maintaining a choice (to have an abortion) for both ourselves and for all those we care about. How would such a bumper-sticker affect a person who opposes abortion because he strongly values life from the moment of conception?

money. Patients might pay more or less for care that is better or worse. People might pay more or less for their insurance. A quick reflection reveals four stakeholders with financial interests: healthcare providers, medical-device manufacturers, patients, and insurance-policy holders. But not all interests are financial. A stakeholder's interests may be aesthetic. Someone owning a house in a neighborhood may care about a building development (a new shopping mall, for example) because it will be ugly or beautiful. And separate interests may overlap. The same person who frets about that unsightly new shopping mall might also worry that her property value will go down once this eyesore is visible from her front yard. When you try to identify stakeholders according to their interests, ask yourself: Who stands to win or lose if this controversy is decided one way or the other? What will this person/organization gain? What might be taken away or reduced? Keep in mind that the interest can be anything that a person or an organization cares about: money, power, beauty, prestige, friends, family.

Values: When we talk about *interests*, we focus on the things that directly affect individuals. When we talk about *values*, we focus on things people care about even when they are not personally or directly affected by those things. I have an interest in my own house and its architecture. But I may value your house and its architecture. I want to protect my house so that I will have a place to live. I may want to protect your house so that the bungalow style of home architecture will live on. You have an interest in your own marriage so that you will have a stable and loving relationship. But you may value the institution of marriage because it has been historically important. An art collector has an interest in a painting he recently acquired. But he may value all art because it embodies creativity. People become stakeholders in controversies not just because they are directly affected (not just because they have an *interest* in its outcome) but also because they *value* something affected by the controversy's outcome. The ongoing controversy about abortion is a great example of a disagreement featuring stakeholders who are principally value-holders. Many of those who care most deeply about abortion—such as Roman Catholic clergy—do not provide abortions, have never had an abortion, and will never have an abortion. But they value life (which they believe begins at conception). Because they value life, they argue against abortion.

Beliefs: Our interests and our values affect our opinions, but so do our beliefs. For instance, right now, in Texas, people are arguing about how to regulate a new method of drilling for natural gas (usually called "fracking" or "hydrofracking"). Those living in areas where this drilling happens are likely to believe that hydrofracking affects the land and the water supply because they have experienced these effects first-hand. Those involved in the industry are likely to believe that hydrofracking is safe because they know the precautions taken while drilling. And those who enforce current regulations are likely to believe that there may be a problem with hydrofracking because they know how many reported violations have occurred. The town resident might have first-hand knowledge of ground tremors and pungent well water. The petroleum engineer might know all the efforts taken to prevent contamination and to monitor seismic activity. The environmental regulator might know of many complaints about tremors and water contamination, but he might also know that the investigations remain inconclusive. The resident, based on her beliefs (and interests and values), may favor stricter regulations. The engineer, based on her beliefs, may oppose any new regulations. And the environmental regulator, based on his experiences, might support *some* new regulations to prevent possible damage that, as of yet, cannot be verified.

While we encourage you to think about stakeholders in terms of their interests, their values, and their beliefs, we caution against any attempt to pigeonhole a stakeholder. When you are trying to identify stakeholders, start with real people. Then ask yourself these questions: What affects this person? What does he care about? What does she believe? And how do these interests, these values, and these beliefs lead him or her to take this position in the controversy? If you can explain one stakeholder's position based on his or her interests, values, and beliefs, then you can predict what similar people might feel or think.

Viewpoints in a Controversy

If you have identified a recent public controversy and you know who the stakeholders are, then you can imagine what their viewpoints will be. But, typically, those trying to map a controversy do not start with profiles of the stakeholders. Instead, they start with viewpoints—the arguments made by stakeholders. And that's what we recommend you do. Once you suspect that there is a controversy, try to find a few viewpoints, such as articles in which people express their opinions.

If you suspect that there is a controversy about capital punishment in Texas, look for opinion articles arguing in favor of and articles arguing against capital punishment. You might find, based on the viewpoints you locate, that such a controversy does exist. Right now, people do argue about capital punishment. You might read a viewpoint article in which one stakeholder (a politician who wants to seem tough on crime) argues in favor of capital punishment. And you might find another article in which another stakeholder (a clergyman who values mercy) argues against it. But through your research you might find that the controversy is not quite what you predicted. Maybe the most recent controversy is not about executing criminals but about executing foreign criminals. In January of 2014, because the state of Texas planned to execute Edgar Tamayo Arias, a Mexican citizen, many argued about whether this execution would constitute a breach of international law. Or you might see that people are debating the manner of execution. Is death by a certain combination of drugs "cruel and unusual punishment"? In April of 2014, as the state prepared to execute Tommy Lynn Sells, many people defended and many attacked lethal injection. The debate became so heated that the state refused to release information about where it got the drug (pentobarbital) used in executions. In 2015, as supplies of pentobarbital were running out, citizens in several states are debating other ways to execute inmates. Some suggestions, such as electric chairs and firing squads, have sparked new and heated controversy. Others, such as new drug combinations, have not.

Concluding Advice about Finding and then Mapping Controversies

The basic lesson to take away is this: You are looking for a recent public controversy with stakeholders who express viewpoints, but you will start by finding viewpoints. Based on these viewpoints, you will determine who the stakeholders are and what the controversy is about. When you have identified a recent public controversy and the viewpoints involved in it, develop a theory or hypothesis. Try to phrase your controversy as a question. And keep in mind that this question is just a hypothesis. People might be arguing about this question. But they might be arguing about something completely different. Only research can determine what people are currently arguing, who's arguing, and why they're taking certain positions.

Brief Exercise: In ancient Rome, students attended "rhetoric" schools where they learned to argue. In these schools, they completed exercises, just as you are asked to write essays in your classes. And many of these exercises aimed to teach students how to think about controversies. Try this one: Read the following description of a hypothetical, ancient legal case (taken from the writings of Seneca the Elder and represented here as it appears in Jeffrey Walker's *The Genuine Teachers of this Art* [University of South Carolina Press, 2011], pp. 196–197):

> **The Case of the Pirate Chief's Daughter:** A man captured by pirates wrote to his father about a ransom. He was not ransomed. The daughter of the pirate chief made him swear to marry her if he was released. He swore. She left her father and followed the young man. He returned to his father and married the girl. An orphan appears. The father orders his son to divorce the pirate chief's daughter and marry the orphan. The son refuses and is disinherited.

After reading the case description, work with a partner to argue the following viewpoints. Have each person defend one of these stakeholders' interests and values:

- **Stakeholder**: The son. **Viewpoint**: I deserve restitution from my father for the inheritance he took from me.
- **Stakeholder**: The father. **Viewpoint**: I owe my son nothing.

After arguing these viewpoints, invent others based on what you know or can imagine about the other stakeholders. What would the pirate's daughter have to say? What would the orphan claim? Act out your arguments in a mock courtroom setting, with specific people playing the parts of advocates, others the parts of witnesses. Appoint a jury. Let them rule on the case. And, most importantly, appoint court reporters who must explain to those outside the courtroom what this controversy is really about, who the stakeholders are, and what viewpoints they expressed.

Short Writing Assignment : To kick-start your research into a recent public controversy, come up with a hypothetical controversy. Try to phrase your description of the controversy as a question using one (or more) of the following templates:

- Should we do _____?
- What effects will _____ have on _____ people?
- Should we believe that _____ is good/right/just/fair [pick one or insert your own]?
- Is _____ good/right/just/fair because it has or lacks the following good effects _____?
- Is _____ good/right/just/fair because it embodies/relates to _____, which we also care about or which we do not like at all?
- Is _____ good/right/just/fair because future generations will benefit/ appreciate or suffer from _____?
- Should we value and protect _____ by doing _____?
- Should we understand that _____ is true or false because of _____?
- Should we not do _____ because we don't know enough yet?
- Should we learn more about _____ so that we don't end up doing _____?

Once you have your controversy phrased as a question, speculate about the stakeholders and the viewpoints they are likely to take. For example:

Controversy: Should we abolish the death penalty?

Stakeholder 1: Politicians who are tough on crime will say we should execute criminals because it effectively deters crime.

Stakeholder 2: Defense lawyers who are concerned about executing innocent people will say we should not execute criminals because we might kill an innocent person.

Stakeholder 3: Citizens worried about taxes will say we should abolish the death penalty because it is costly and ineffective.

Stakeholder 4: Victims and their families will say we should keep the death penalty to make sure heinous criminals get punished appropriately.

After you've phrased your controversy as a question and speculated about who the stakeholders are and what they'll say, read over your answers and circle the terms that appear most often or that seem most important. Looking at the above description of a hypothetical controversy, the following terms stand out: "death penalty," "capital punishment," "execute," "innocent," "justice," "victims," and "ineffective." These are keywords—whenever we hear them together, there's a good chance people are debating capital punishment. Your keywords will help you find real articles about your controversy or a related controversy.

CHAPTER 1 | Finding and Evaluating Viewpoints

If you have a potential controversy and you've thought about the possible stakeholders and their positions, then you are ready to begin your research. In this chapter, we will introduce you to some basic tools for finding information. We will also help you to evaluate your research. Before we do, however, we'd like to make a few points about research in general:

- Research, like writing, is something you do over and over again. You don't research once and then write. You research, write, research some more, write some more, research a bit more, write a bit more, and so on.
- Research is not just the process of finding information. It's also the process of evaluating information. As you research, you must decide what is good or bad, useful or not.
- Research requires looking through a range of sources to find different kinds of information.
- Research generally begins with questions and keywords.

If you haven't developed a list of keywords, we recommend that you return to the end of the introductory chapter and complete the "Short Writing Assignment" presented there. It will help you develop a list of keywords. The UT library also offers an exercise that will help you develop a list of keywords; you can find it at: http://www.lib.utexas. edu/keywords/. Try either or both exercises. Most importantly, don't start looking for sources until you've found some keywords that can guide your research.

Finding Information

To introduce the basics of research, let's explore three tools: the search engine, the database, and the encyclopedia. Each leads to a different kind of information.

Search Engines
You are likely familiar with search engines because most regular Internet users employ these tools every day. It is important to keep in mind that Internet search engines contain no sources. They point to sources. Once you've done a Google search, for instance, you must click on a link that seems relevant to your search terms. The link

takes you somewhere else, somewhere other than the Google search engine or the Google search page. Something else to keep in mind about Internet search engines: They lead to information that has not been *curated*.

Since we will use this term a lot, allow us a moment to define it. When someone *curates* information, he or she organizes it for an audience. That's why we say that a museum "curates" its collection of historical or artistic artifacts. A bunch of unorganized fossils on a table would make no sense to someone who is not a paleontologist. Someone at the natural science museum curates these fossils by putting them in displays that include explanations of where they were found, which animals they belonged to, and when these animals probably lived. Curated information is more accessible, but it is also more

Brief Exercise: Take your keywords and apply the following techniques for limiting searches in Google. Keep careful track of how the search results differ. (This exercise is adapted from http://tinyurl.com/d83ho7o and http://tinyurl.com/d354vw8. To learn even more about searching Google, we suggest visiting the original tutorials.)

- Search for an exact phrase by placing that phrase in quotation marks.
    - Example: "ten percent rule"
- Exclude a word by placing a dash (–) in front of the word.
    - Example: vegetarianism – health
    - This command will find results that include the word *vegetarianism* but not the word *health*.
- Place a tilde (~) before a word to search for similar words.
    - Example: ~ teacher salaries
    - This command will find results that include synonyms for teacher (such as *educator* or *instructor*) and that include the word salaries.
- Search for multiple alternative words by placing OR between the words.
    - Example: vegetarianism health OR environment
    - This command will find results about vegetarianism that also contain the word *health* or the word *environment*.
- Search for results within a specific date range by placing ellipses (…) between the dates.
    - Example: global warming 2010…2013
- Search for results on a specific site or kind of site by using "site:" and a domain descriptor.
    - Example: global warming site:edu
    - Example: free speech site:aclu.org

You can use these Google tricks in combination as well. For example, if you are looking for results about Internet privacy that are not about Facebook and that appeared on .org sites in the past three years, your search term might look like this: site:.org ~Internet privacy -Facebook 2010…2014 limited. Uncurated information is more plentiful but less helpful. Searching Google to find articles about race and criminal justice is a bit like walking into a room filled with a disorganized pile of all the fossils in all the world. You might find the T-Rex you're looking for—if you know what to look for—but you'll have to sort through a bunch of other rocks in the process.

An Internet search engine can be a good place to start your research. To pick up an example from the last chapter, if you type "race conscious admissions University of Texas" into Google, you may get a bunch of links to arguments supporting and/or opposing UT's policy on race-conscious admissions. And if you do get such links, then you definitely have a controversy. But you will also get many other links—links to articles about the legal case that Abigail Fisher filed against UT, for instance, will be plentiful. Uncurated information comes in all shapes and sizes. But you can limit the information that you receive, and you can more effectively search Google by using a few basic tricks of database searching. Since Google is one of (if not the) most popular Internet search engines in the U.S., we'll demonstrate ways to limit searches using Google. But keep in mind that every Internet search engine can limit searches in these ways, even though every Internet search engine may not use the same commands.

After searching the Internet for a little while, you will likely have a better understanding of what's out there. If none of your searches brings you to any recent arguments about your controversy, then you may need to rephrase the controversy, rethink the keywords, or simply choose another (hopefully related) controversy. If everything goes very well, you will have links to recent articles in which stakeholders express their opinions regarding your chosen controversy.

No matter what the outcome, do not limit yourself to using only search engines— whether you use Google and/or any other search engine. This is important for a several reasons. First, Internet search engines do not discriminate among information sources. Every source, at a glance, appears equally believable and equally useful. Second, Internet searches do not give access to information that you have to pay for. A lot of information belongs to a person or organization, and you can't access it without paying a fee. Sometimes you can't even find it without paying for access. Finally, Internet searches link only to *online media*, the stuff that's on the web. A lot of information may be primarily offered in a different *medium*, such as print. In sum, Google will help you to find blogs (some written by reliable sources, some not) that are free to read online. Google may help you to find articles that appear online or both online and in print. But other research tools will help you find other—and potentially more useful—sources in different media.

Databases
A database is a collection of information. It will include a search engine, but this search engine will point you only to information that is housed in the database. Databases are typically *proprietary*—someone owns each database and will not allow you to use it until you pay a fee and have permission. Each database contains a specific kind of

information. For instance, some databases—such as those of the Modern Language Association (MLA) or the Education Resources and Information Center (ERIC)—list titles and abstracts of articles. If you want to find the complete article, you must go elsewhere, probably to a library with a subscription to the journal that published the article. Some databases, on the other hand, include the full text of the articles. All databases curate the information to some degree. MLA, for example, features only articles from academic journals in certain humanities disciplines: English, literature, foreign languages, and the like.

A database has several advantages over an Internet search engine. Database searches allow you to focus on a particular kind and a particular quality of information. You are trying to map a recent public controversy, so you are looking for credible sources in recent media. You want to read, among other things, arguments about pressing issues. Such articles tend to appear in newspapers or magazines, on TV news programs, and on particular websites. Such articles tend to be credible when they are published by nationally recognized and respected venues, such as the *Wall Street Journal, New York Times, Salon,* and *HumanEventsOnline.* So you want a database that focuses on a certain subject (current events), on certain media (both digital and print), and on certain venues (news outlets).

Since we know what kind of research you will be doing, we can recommend a few databases that you will find useful:

- Alt-Press Watch (a collection of articles from "alternative" media)
- Ethnic News Watch (a collection of articles from ethnic, minority, and native press outlets)
- Factiva (a collection of articles about business and finance)
- Academic OneFile (a database that features scholarly and newspaper articles on current events)
- Academic Search Complete (like Academic OneFile, this database features scholarly and popular sources about current events)
- LexisNexis (a collection of articles and other news media from a range of sources)

Three things are important to note here. First, since the above are all *proprietary* databases, you must access them through the UT library website. UT pays for access, allowing you to log in to and search these databases only if you go through the UT portal (lib.utexas.edu) and use your UT EID. Second, each database has its own peculiar search interface, so you will have to learn how to search each one (your instructor or a librarian can help you with this), but they do share features, and they all use keywords. Third, each of these databases leads to a different kind of information, so you may want to search all six to find everything you possibly can.

We believe that LexisNexis will be the most useful to you, so the UT librarians have provided a helpful tutorial on searching this database: http://www.lib.utexas.edu/students/find/lexisnexistips.html

This tutorial will help you to locate opinion (viewpoint) articles—exactly the sort of thing you're looking for. Later in this chapter, we will discuss the difference between viewpoint and information articles. For now, try searching in each of the databases. See how database searching differs from Internet searching.

Database searching is a good second step in your research process. After you've searched the Internet to get a feel for your controversy and to find a couple of potentially useful sources, you can go into the databases and find even more useful and more credible sources.

Encyclopedias

An encyclopedia may be the oldest (or at least one of the oldest) ways to curate information. Encyclopedias were around in ancient Greece, and you can still find them today. An encyclopedia is an effort to collect and condense everything we know—in general or about a particular subject, e.g., an encyclopedia of philosophy. Of course, no one can collect or present all knowledge. So encyclopedias summarize and excerpt. They give brief introductions to topics, and they reprint or summarize parts of various sources. The most commonly used online encyclopedia today is Wikipedia, a compendium of information composed by the users themselves. Wikipedia users add information, oftentimes linking to their sources to show us that they have done their homework. Like most encyclopedias, Wikipedia is a great source for background information—terms, dates, and events that you don't know or understand.

Wikipedia is an "open-source" encyclopedia—almost anyone can contribute, and everyone has access. Here are a couple of *proprietary* encyclopedias that might come in handy during your research:

- Gale Virtual Reference Library
- Opposing Viewpoints

You can find descriptions of and advice about using each on the following UT library webpage: http://www.lib.utexas.edu/services/instruction/rhe/findbackinfo.html

Encyclopedias are the research tools you want to keep always at your side

Further Discussion: Read a Wikipedia entry on a recent controversial topic, such as immigration reform or handgun regulation. Then consult another encyclopedia—such as the Gale Virtual Library or Opposing Viewpoints—on the same subject. What terms (keywords) appear in both? What background information—history, definitions, key concepts—do they both offer the reader? Based on the common keywords, how would you change the way you're searching for articles? Based on the common background information, what will you have to teach an interested but uninformed audience about your controversy before you begin to summarize the viewpoints in the controversy?

Brief Exercise: We discuss Internet search engines, databases, and encyclopedias in terms of the media they tend to feature, the kind of information they privilege, and the levels of curation they offer. Using the following chart, describe a couple of other more recent research tools. Fill in the empty boxes in the last two rows of this table:

Research Tool	Privileged Media	Kind of Information	Level of Curation
Wikipedia	Digital	Summary articles	Heavy
Google	Digital	All kinds	None
LexisNexis	Print	Newspaper articles	Somewhat
Reddit.com			
Yahoo News			

How do these new research tools stack up against those we discussed earlier? Are they more like Internet search engines, databases, or encyclopedias? Or are they something else altogether? Are they useful to someone researching a controversy?

but never at the center of your work. They help you to make sense of a new subject; and they might point you to new sources by introducing keywords or even by linking to a source. But you should not rely on encyclopedias for anything else, for two reasons: First, you want to see the information first-hand. Encyclopedias are so heavily curated that you cannot get the most recent or even the most important information from them. So you must go to the original sources—the people who first offered the ideas and opinions that encyclopedias reference. Second, experienced researchers know that encyclopedias are not the most up-to-date, the most relevant, or the most comprehensive sources. Encyclopedia entries are rarely written by experts, and they're never written for specialists, so they tend to feature basic concepts. That's why journalists and your professors chuckle when they read an article that relies heavily on Wikipedia for information. Wikipedia is a good start, but it should not be the end of your journey. If Wikipedia is your ultimate source, if it's the first and the last thing you consult, then a knowledgeable audience will suspect that you are not knowledgeable yourself.

Evaluating Information

Once you find a bunch of potentially useful sources, you will have to decide which will be most helpful to your work. We suggest finding more articles than you need because we suspect that some of what you find will not be useful. If your instructor requires that you cite at least three sources, try to find eight or even ten. Then you can start evaluating those sources.

Of course, the most basic way to evaluate information is to say that it is good or it is bad. But since you will be finding many articles produced by news organizations, you will quickly learn that people have very different opinions about what is a good and what is a bad source. Often, people dislike a venue because they disagree with the political perspective of the editorial staff. Since the *New York Times* often publishes editorials with a liberal bias, some conservatives think it's a poor source of information. And since the *Wall Street Journal* tends to publish editorials with a conservative bias, some liberals think it's a poor source of information. Both news organizations are, by the way, leaders in the industry. People most able to recognize good journalism—journalists—hold both venues in high esteem. Try to avoid evaluating a source based on the political bias it demonstrates. Focus on the source's credibility instead: Is the information well-researched? Is the writer an expert? Is the venue respected by people who know this subject?

Further Discussion: The UT library offers a helpful table of databases that should lead you to credible viewpoint sources. We encourage you to take a look:

http://www.lib.utexas.edu/students/find/findoped.html

The above link takes you to a long webpage. At the bottom of this page, note the table that classifies venues according to their political bias: some as conservative, some as liberal. Click through to the websites. Does each news organization seem credible, even though it's biased? Why or why not?

Viewpoint and Information Articles

While researching a controversy, the most important distinction that you must draw is between a viewpoint source and an information source. In the early days of modern journalism, this was a hard distinction to make because newspapers mixed commentary with reporting. An article would tell its audience about recent events while also trying to convince them to believe or feel something about these events. News articles offered both a viewpoint and information. Through most of the twentieth century, however, newspapers and magazines tried to separate viewpoints from information by offering information articles in one section and opinions and editorials in another. That is why when you pick up a newspaper or go to a newspaper's website, you'll see a section titled "Opinions and Editorials." That's the viewpoint section, the place where people get to argue their beliefs. The rest of the articles are supposed to offer information alone.

Information articles often tell the reader about people's viewpoints, but they do so by quoting or summarizing and always by *attributing* the viewpoint to someone. The reporter will write, for instance, "According to Representative Cushman (Republican from Oklahoma), the healthcare.gov website is a 'train wreck.'" Information articles try to stay unbiased by offering at least two viewpoints on any controversial issue. So to avoid inserting her own opinion or slant, the reporter who wrote the sentence above would quickly provide another viewpoint attributed to another stakeholder: "But Democrats and the White House believe that the website, despite its initial troubles, is working very well. 'There were a few hiccups at first,' said Jane Johnson (Democrat from Illinois), 'but healthcare.gov is now up and running.'"

Unfortunately, when you find news articles in a database, you may not know which section of the magazine or newspaper these articles first appeared in, so you may have trouble determining what kind of article you're reading. Here are a few clues to look for.

Viewpoint articles:
- Use the first and the second person: "When I see the DOW average fall, I conclude that the U.S. economy is struggling."
- Express ideas—opinions, beliefs, and factual claims—without attributing them to someone else: "Global warming is really happening, faster than we think, and because of human-made carbon emissions."
- Include strong language designed to move the audience: "Continuing to give food stamps to *undeserving* people who trade them for drugs and liquor will not help anyone and will *certainly lead to the crippling dependency that plagues our inner cities.*"
- Tend to put the background information in the middle of the article, pushing the arguments up to the front where they will get more attention.

Information articles:
- Use the third person, unless quoting: "If stock values on the DOW and the NASDAQ averages are any indication, then the U.S. economy is struggling."
- Attribute ideas—opinions, beliefs, and factual claims—to other people: "John Finglehopper, a climatologist at the University of Northeast State, said at a recent demonstration against drilling for oil along the U.S. Gulf Coast, 'Global warming is really happening, faster than we think, and because of human-made carbon emissions.'"
- Avoid strong language and instead use words to qualify claims: "A study by the Omnibus Foundation reports that *some* people trade food stamps for *illegal narcotics* and *alcohol.* The study concludes that food stamps may allow some people to stay on public support longer than necessary and *may also contribute to systemic urban poverty.*"
- Tend to put background information near the end and new information at the beginning, so the audience will focus on the new developments.

Unfortunately, you will find that much journalism in the U.S. does not follow these standards very strictly. Many news sources, nowadays, mix viewpoints and information together, making the researcher's job much more difficult. A news site like Salon. com will feature many articles that both express opinions and give information. News networks such as Fox and MSNBC flip back and forth between opinion and information. For this reason, we encourage you to consider three categories of news media: information sources, viewpoint sources, and info-argument sources. Be especially careful of the info-arguments. In the middle of an information article about a Supreme Court case, you may find a harangue against the justices who wrote the majority decision. And the writer may not tell you explicitly that he's finished reporting what other people think and has begun to tell you what he thinks.

You need to learn and present information about your controversy while summarizing the viewpoints of its stakeholders. So you should look for both information and viewpoint articles. And you should also accept info-arguments. Finally, you should notice when information shades into opinion. Your job is to separate the information from the opinion for your audience. Tell us what has happened in the controversy (information). Tell us who the stakeholders are (more information). Tell us what they have said (viewpoints). If you can identify a handful of sources, written by different stakeholders, as unquestionably viewpoint articles, then you should reference these sources when summarizing the important stakeholders' beliefs. Reference the rest—the information and the info-arguments—as background information to show your audience what the controversy is, why it matters, and what has led the stakeholders to take these particular positions.

Credible Sources

When considering either information or viewpoint sources, it's important to evaluate the writers' credibility. Should these people be trusted? Are they experts? Have they done enough research? Are they stretching the truth?

We warn you against equating credibility with bias. These are two different and equally important qualities. A writer's bias is his or her inclination to believe a particular perspective. I may be liberally biased because I'm a Democrat, and you may be conservatively biased because you're a Republican. But, despite our opposing biases, we can both be credible because we can both research our topics thoroughly. We can present our arguments honestly. And we can treat each other fairly. A credible source is one you can trust because

- He or she is knowledgeable.
- He or she has your or the community's best interests at heart.
- He or she treats others—even stakeholders with opposite viewpoints—respectfully.

Here are some things to consider when judging a writer's credibility:

- **Is the writer a recognized expert?** What is the writer's stake in making this argument? Does the writer have expertise in the area so that he or she can write an informed viewpoint? Is this viewpoint representative—can this person speak credibly for a larger group?
- **If the writer is not an expert, does the writer cite expert sources?** Does the author cite anyone at all? Do the author's sources have sufficient expertise to make his or her statements believable?
- **What is the venue, and who is the audience?** Who was the piece written for? In what source was it published? Would you expect the audience to be informed and reasonable? Does the venue tend to publish carefully researched and substantial arguments?

- **How strong is the writer's argument?** How is the argument supported? What kind of evidence does the writer use?
- **How accurate is the writer's information?** Does the writer cite sources? (A lack of citation or attribution is often a sign that someone is hiding poor research.) Is this evidence credible and accurate? Is the evidence from biased sources?
- **How does the writer address his or her opposition?** A credible source will represent the opposing opinions fairly and will respectfully explain why she disagrees. Does this writer oversimplify the opinions of opponents so that these opinions can be easily refuted? Does the writer make fun of or dismiss opponents or their ideas?
- **How current is the writer's information?** Does the writer rely on the most up-to-date information?

Source Bias

Since you're looking for viewpoint articles, many of your sources will be biased. Viewpoint articles are written by stakeholders to convince others that a particular perspective is best. Your job is not to show your reader *that* a piece is biased. Your job is to think about *how* and *why* it's biased. Understanding a source's bias will help you to make sense of the controversy. Once you can identify the source's bias, you'll be able to discern why some stakeholders tend to favor this viewpoint. When reflecting on a source's bias, you may have to learn about the writer. Does this person belong to an institution or an industry that accounts for his bias? Further research into the venue or the audience will also help. Does this magazine typically publish arguments that appeal to a specific political leaning? Here are few things to consider when thinking about bias:

- **Writer**: Who is the writer? What is the writer's stake in making this argument? (Note that "editorials" published in magazines and newspapers don't list a writer because the audience will assume that the arguments presented reflect the bias of the publication's editorial staff. If you want to find out whether the *Washington Post*—or any other venue—has a liberal or a conservative bias, read the editorials.)
- **Venue**: Who is the audience? Where is this published? What does that tell you, if anything, about the perspective?
- **Alternative Views**: How, if at all, does the writer recognize and address opposing viewpoints? A writer who opposes a particular viewpoint is likely biased against that perspective. A writer who strongly opposes a particular viewpoint, to the point of deriding the opposition, is certainly biased.
- **Language**: Does the author use language that indicates one viewpoint in a controversy? People who favor legalizing marijuana tend to call it "cannabis." People who oppose capital punishment tend to call it the "death penalty." Often, people expressing opposing viewpoints in a debate use opposite terms: "pro-life" vs. "pro-choice"; "death tax" vs. "estate tax"; "illegal alien" vs. "undocumented immigrant." These keywords not only allow you to identify bias, but they will also help you to search for other, similar viewpoints.

Short Writing Assignment—Research Log: Keep a research log, a record of
where you've searched, what search terms you used, and what you found. For every
search, record the following information: tool, keywords, parameters, results. For
example:

Research Tool	Keywords	Parameters	Results
Google	illegal immigration texas fence	typed into the search box with no punctuation	An article on Forbes.com (7-18-2013), arguing that the fence is too costly
Google	texas border fence	typed into the search box with no punctuation	An article from *The Lookout*, 12-21-2011 (hosted on *Yahoo News*) about U.S. citizens who will live in U.S. territory that is on the Mexican side of the fence. A blog dedicated to opposing the border fence: notexasborderwall
LexisNexis	texas border fence	Typed into search box with no punctuation, searching "all news" from April 1, 2013–April 7, 2013, and exclusively collecting editorials and opinions	A May 15, 2013, article from the *Augusta Chronicle* about an immigration bill introduced by Marco Rubio. The article includes the phrase "Texas border fence" but does not discuss the fence itself.
LexisNexis	texas fence	Typed into search box with no punctuation, searching "all news" for all dates and exclusively collecting editorials and opinions	A May 4, 2008, *New York Times* article arguing against the fence along the Texas border.

After you've done a few searches using different keywords, different parameters,
and different research tools, answer the following questions:

- Which search terms lead you to the most relevant results?
- Which search terms and databases reliably lead to information sources?
  Viewpoint sources?
- Which search terms and databases lead you to credible sources?
- Which search terms and databases lead you to sources with particular biases?
- How will you alter your research techniques, your controversy, and/or your list of
  keywords based on what you've found so far?

CHAPTER

2 | Summarizing Sources

Summarizing what other people have said is one of the most important writing skills that you can learn in your first year of college. In school and elsewhere, you will spend a lot of time telling some people what other people believe. In college classes, you'll have to tell your professors what experts say. In professional settings, you'll have to explain to your coworkers what experienced professionals do. In public writing, you'll have to say what other citizens believe. Even in scientific reports, when presenting a completely new discovery, you will have to summarize existing "literature" to show why your discovery is relevant to other people's primary research. Effective writing is always situated in a conversation. Writing that contributes to a conversation appears interesting and relevant. If you cannot situate your writing in a conversation, then you will talk to yourself. And that kind of conversation interests only one person.

In this chapter, we will introduce you to some basic principles and practices of summarization. We do so in order to prepare you to map a controversy. However, summary skills will be useful to you long after you've finished this assignment. Our introduction will prepare you to map your controversy, and it will also prepare you for other writing challenges that you will encounter after this class is completed.

Selecting

Summaries condense information by leaving some ideas out. When mapping a controversy, you will have to select the information that best shows your readers why and how people disagree. Deciding what is most important, however, can be difficult. The "most important" information can be found by asking two questions: (1) What would the writer most want the audience to remember? (2) What do you want to show in your map of the controversy?

Most Important to the writer: Since you cannot directly ask the writer of an article what is most important to him or her, you have to look at the source itself. Certain features in the writing will signal importance. Writers make important information stand out. Look for these qualities that most writers will give to important information:

- Important ideas are often found in the title or subtitle of an article.

- Important ideas are often at the beginning and/or end of an argument, the parts that the reader is likely to remember. If an idea appears both at the beginning and at the end, it is certainly important.
- Important ideas are often stated very directly in short, clear sentences.
- Important ideas follow a phrase or sentence that indicates a conclusion: "Based on my experiences, I feel that… "; "Our research leads us to conclude …"; "The data demonstrate…"; "The above analysis proves…"

In a very complex argument, the author may bluntly state her principal claim and then summarize the reasons that should lead the audience to accept that claim. For example: "The U.S. tax code is overly complicated and can be replaced with something simpler and more effective [**the writer's principal claim**]. I will demonstrate, first, by exploring some of the needless complexities that you can see in your own income-tax return forms [**the first reason that supports the claim**]. Then, I will compare our system of collecting income taxes to the much simpler and more effective systems in two other countries [**the second reason that supports the claim**]. Finally, I will point to the income-tax laws in New York, Arizona, and North Dakota to show that some of our own states have recognized the problem and have begun to explore its solutions [**the third reason that supports the claim**]." Later in this book, we will discuss this kind of "partition" in greater detail.

For now, while we encourage you to look for such statements, we also want you to understand that writers don't always say what they're going to say. Sometimes, especially when writing to an audience who are likely to disagree, a writer will wait until the end—after she's explained her reasons. For instance, "It's time to file your income-tax return forms, and you may have noticed that explaining to the government what you owe is quite complicated." After such an introduction, the writer can explain that income-tax complexities are not present in other countries. And then, the writer can explain that many states, in their local income-tax forms, have done away with these complex formulas. Finally, the writer can reveal her main claim, in the conclusion: "If our income-tax forms are so complicated, and other countries and states have found ways to simplify this process, why can't the U.S. government do the same?" But notice that this last sentence doesn't directly state the writer's principal claim. The question lets you arrive at the conclusion. You're supposed to answer the question, "Yes, of course, the U.S. government can simplify the process!" Our brief example is meant to illustrate a very simple but important point: Some writers *explicitly* state their principal claims. Others *implicitly* suggest what they want the audience to conclude. Here are strategies for identifying the principal claims in both *explicit* and *implicit* arguments.

While you're looking at an *explicit* argument:
- Underline one or two sentences that clearly and directly state what the writer wants the audience to remember, the writer's principal *claim*: "The U.S. tax code is overly complicated and can be replaced with something simpler and more effective."

- Underline or label the chief *reasons* that the writer gives to convince the audience that they should believe the principal claim: (1) There are "needless complexities that you can see in your own income-tax return forms"; (2) Two other countries have "much simpler and more effective systems"; (3) "income-tax laws in New York, Arizona, and North Dakota…show that some of our own states have recognized the problem and have begun to explore its solutions."
- Underline or label the *evidence* that the writer gives to show the audience that these reasons are sound: (1) a detailed explanation of tax laws in two foreign countries; (2) a detailed explanation of simpler tax laws in three U.S. states.

When you've finished looking at an *implicit* argument:
- State in your own words what the writer wants the audience to remember, the writer's principal *claim*. Use these three templates as guides: The writer wants the audience to believe _____. The writer wants the audience to feel _____. The writer wants the audience to do _____. For instance: *The writer wants the audience to believe* that the U.S. tax system is too complicated. *The writer wants the audience to feel* frustrated by their tax laws. *The writer wants the audience to do* something about (change) the U.S. tax code.
- State in your own words what *reasons* the audience should consider. Start your own summary sentence with the words "because" or "since," and then restate the reason; follow with "the audience should believe/feel/do," and then restate the writer's claim. For instance: *Since* [**reason**] their income-tax forms are frustratingly difficult, *the audience should believe* [**claim**] that the U.S. tax system is itself unnecessarily complicated.
- State in your own words what information (what evidence) the writer provides to support each reason. Start these summary sentences with the words "to show the audience that" and then restate the reason; follow with "the writer provides/explains/demonstrates" and restate the evidence. For instance, *To show the audience that* their income-tax forms are frustratingly difficult [**reason**], *the writer explains* the procedure for claiming and paying taxes on income earned as a consultant but not taxed at the point of payment [**evidence**].

Before moving on to the strategies for identifying the information that is most important to you, allow us to more fully explain the difference between *explicit* and *implicit* arguments and why this difference matters so much when you are summarizing a source.

It is easier to summarize *explicit* arguments because the writer labels his *claims*, his *reasons*, and his *evidence*. He tells you what you should believe or feel or do. Then he tells you why you should believe or feel or do this. Finally, he shows you what information you should consider in order to understand why you should believe or feel or do this. *Implicit* arguments lay everything out before the audience, and they let us sort the principal claims from the reasons and the reasons from the evidence. Usually, without even thinking about it, we figure it out. If we don't figure it out, we leave confused and frustrated. If we do figure it out, we feel like we arrived at the conclusions ourselves, so we are more likely to believe. Here, you can see one of the key differences between *explicit* and *implicit* arguments, from a reader's perspective. *Explicit* arguments are clear, direct, but less convincing because they tell the reader what to believe (and nobody likes to be told what to do). *Implicit* arguments are less clear, indirect, but more convincing because they let us arrive at the conclusions ourselves (and we tend to believe conclusions that we have reached ourselves).

When you are summarizing an argument, you must make everything *explicit* for your reader. You should, therefore, present every argument—even the *implicit* ones—*explicitly*. If you *implicitly* summarize a writer's *implicit* claims, reasons, and evidence, you will confuse your reader. Remember, you're mapping a controversy for an interested but uninformed audience. They're reading your essay because they want someone to make sense of a confusing controversy. The clearest map of a controversy will feature explicit summaries of arguments that other people have made. The same is true of any other effort at summarizing. Readers expect summaries to be clear and direct. Readers expect summaries *explicitly* to present all the claims, reasons, and evidence, even the ones that were originally *implicitly* argued. That's why we encourage you to identify the information that is most important to the writer, and explicitly present it to your reader.

Most Important to you: To emphasize the information that you think important, you may have to summarize the argument a bit differently from the way you found it. Making an implicit argument explicit is one such change; the writer chose to make the argument implicitly and, in order to clarify the argument for your audience, you decide to restate its claims, reasons, and evidence explicitly. It's okay to make such changes so long as you write *fair* and *accurate* summaries.

Why would you alter a writer's presentation of her argument? Perhaps you want to emphasize a point of disagreement in the controversy. We have used the terms "claims," "reasons," and "evidence" in this section to discuss the parts of an argument. Writers are always most concerned with their principal claims. The reasons and evidence are there to make the audience accept the claims. But, when summarizing the controversy, you may notice that two people arrive at the same claim through different reasons. As a result, when you summarize the two arguments, you will briefly explain the common claims that both writers want to emphasize: "Both Eugene and Tixelbottom believe that the city police should do more to stop bicycle theft." And you may emphasize their different reasons to illustrate the disagreement. Eugene spends one paragraph explaining that bike theft is a serious crime comparable to automobile theft, and then he spends three paragraphs talking about how much bike theft inconveniences cyclists. Tixelbottom writes a twelve-paragraph essay about how bike theft hurts local bike shops because people buy stolen bikes on the black market rather than new bikes from legal vendors. In your summary, however, you spend one paragraph summarizing each of these contrasting reasons: one paragraph summarizing Eugene, who says bike theft is just like auto theft, and one paragraph summarizing Tixelbottom, who says

Further Discussion: What does it mean to *unfairly* or *inaccurately* summarize a source? You *unfairly* present someone's beliefs when you do not sufficiently show the writer's evidence or her reasons. Let's imagine, for instance, that you are summarizing two sources, one arguing that second-trimester abortions should be legal in the state of Texas and the other claiming that these medical procedures should be illegal. If you show all the evidence and all the reasons to support the first argument but little of the evidence and few of the reasons to support the second argument, then you will make the argument in favor of a law outlawing second-trimester abortions seem weak. You will be treating the argument for outlawing third-trimester abortions unfairly.

You *inaccurately* summarize an argument when you distort the writer's principal claims or her reasons. For instance, let's imagine that the writer who wants to outlaw second-trimester abortions has stated his beliefs this way: "Partial-birth abortions kill a baby who can live on his or her own, outside the mother's womb. It is therefore no different from killing a child moments after a premature delivery. If it is against the law to murder a premature baby, then it should be against the law to abort a pregnancy after three months." You could *unfairly* restate the writer's claim in a couple of ways: **Distorting the claim:** "Edwards thinks that the life of a three-month-old fetus is more important than the health of its mother. He wants to take away a medical procedure that can save a mother's life." **Distorting the reasons:** "Edwards believes that late-term abortion should be made illegal because he thinks that all life is equally sacred." In the first case, as you can see, the summary attributes to the writer a claim that he never made. In the second case, the summary fairly summarizes the writer's claim but then unfairly presents the reason—Edwards never said that "all life" is "equally sacred"; he said Texas murder statutes value the life of a premature newborn and the life of an adult equally.

Try to find, in your own research, an unfair or inaccurate summary of someone else's beliefs. Do you trust the writer who unfairly presents what someone else has said? How could you rewrite the summary to make it fairer or more accurate?

bike theft takes sales away from local bike shops. Obviously, these writers did not intend for their competing reasons to be equally weighted. But, in order to highlight a disagreement, you've summarized these reasons as equally important. As long as you treat these sources fairly and accurately, you should have nothing to worry about. And by emphasizing a point of disagreement, you're able to show your audience that there is a controversy here, even among those who want the same policy: Bike owners feel bike theft is terrible because it harms the bike owners; bike shop owners feel bike theft is terrible because it hurts their business and the local economy.

Since you are trying to map a controversy, you should emphasize the points of agreement or disagreement among stakeholders. Your effort to emphasize these disagreements and agreements may lead you to emphasize contrasting or comparable bits of evidence, common or opposing reasons, or even similar and dissimilar claims. By emphasizing the claims, reasons, and evidence—the information most important to you—you may focus on elements that the writers did not emphasize so strongly. That's okay, so long as your summaries remain fair and accurate. When considering what information you will find important, therefore, we encourage you to look for points of agreement and disagreement. Use the following questions as guides:

- What common claims do stakeholders share? What are the most prevalent opposing claims in this controversy? Often, opposing claims result in opposing proposals for action—outlaw second-trimester abortion; keep second-trimester abortion legal. If you come across such a difference in proposed action, you certainly have opposing claims. But sometimes, opposing claims are more about values—Katy Perry is a sellout, and Adele is a true artist; both Katy Perry and Adele are commercial musicians, both sellouts.
- What common reasons do the stakeholders present? Do stakeholders who arrive at the same claim offer different reasons? Do stakeholders who arrive at different claims sometimes put forward the same reasons? Or do differing claims rely consistently on different reasons? Keeping in mind that a controversy may feature stakeholders who want the same thing but for different reasons, you should closely compare the reasons and the claims that stakeholders offer.
- What evidence do the stakeholders present to convince their audiences of their reasons? Does everyone cite the same example, the same report, or the same expert authority? Do stakeholders arguing contrasting claims tend to cite different kinds of evidence? It is less common to find controversies in which people agree about their claims and reasons but disagree about their evidence, but every so often disagreements about evidence happen. And you should look for them.

Further Discussion: In the first chapter, we mentioned that gender equality is an ongoing controversy. Recently, people have focused on the "gender pay gap," arguing over what causes women to earn less than men (on average), despite equal levels of education and ability. A few people argue that the pay gap is a "myth." But many others agree that the pay gap exists. And they agree that something should be done about it. But they disagree about what causes the pay gap. Do women tend to make less because they choose to spend time at home with their families instead of pursuing career advancement? Or do women tend to select career paths that pay less (nursing and teaching, for example)? Or is there some kind of sexism (conscious or otherwise) that leads managers and decision-makers to award men more than women? And how should we address the pay gap? Legislation that allows women to sue more easily for wage discrimination? Scholarships that encourage women to enter professions with high salaries? More generous maternity leave and support for childcare? Discuss the different viewpoints in this controversy. How would you explain the points of agreement and the points of disagreement?

Contextualizing

For a moment, let's think about what happens when you repeat another person's ideas. First, you choose the most important information, sometimes emphasizing things that the speaker would not emphasize. We've already discussed that process under the heading "Selecting." Then you take that information out of its original context. In context, it's much easier to understand someone, because you can tell who's talking, what that person is responding to, and what has prompted him or her to speak. Out of context, ideas can seem wild, random, and confusing. Therefore, to avoid confusing your reader, you must contextualize your sources. Who is the speaker? What event prompted this person to speak? What is this argument responding to? Sometimes you can do all of this in one sentence. Before offering a quote, you can quickly give biographical information about the writer or quickly explain what the writer is

Brief Exercise: Try contextualizing a source using the following templates:

- **Use a noun phrase or noun clause to introduce the speaker:** [Name of the speaker], [noun phrase describing the speaker], says, "[quote]." For example: Edwin Edgars, a professor of geosciences at the University of West Western, said, "The Earth is getting warmer due to increased carbon dioxide released by volcanic activity. We cannot control this."
- **Use a prepositional phrase to identify the place where the speaker said something**: [Name of speaker], [preposition (*at, in*)] + [description of place], says, "[quote]." For example: Edwin Edgars, at a recent UN summit on global climate change, said, "The Earth is getting warmer due to increased carbon dioxide released by volcanic activity. We cannot control this."
- **Introduce the person to whom or the argument to which the speaker was responding, using a gerund phrase:** [Name of speaker], responding to + [description of the argument to which the speaker was responding], said, "[quote]." For example: Edwin Edgars, responding to another speaker who attributed global warming entirely to human behavior, said, "The Earth is getting warmer due to increased carbon dioxide released by volcanic activity. We cannot control this."
- **Introduce the speaker, the place, and the position addressed, using two prefatory sentences that come before the quote.** [One sentence in which you describe the speaker and the place where the quote was delivered]. [A second sentence in which you describe the events and the other positions that led the speaker to say this]. [Last name of speaker], said, "[quote]." For example: At a recent UN summit on global climate change, renowned geoscientist Edwin Edgars delivered the keynote address. All were gathered to learn about higher levels of greenhouse gases in the Earth's atmosphere, yet Edgars began his talk by responding to those who attribute this recent increase entirely to human behavior. Edgars said, "The Earth is getting warmer due to increased carbon dioxide released by volcanic activity. We cannot control this."

responding to. But sometimes, you need to preface your summary with a couple of sentences that contextualize the source.

There are innumerable ways to contextualize a source. We offer a few in this chapter, but we encourage you to look for others. Pick the methods that work best in your particular paragraph or sentence. You don't have to provide exhaustive contextualization for every quote. Often your audience will know who the speaker is, and sometimes they won't need to know why she's saying something or who she's responding to. Offer the contextualizing information that will help your audience make sense of the summary. Present the information as elegantly and as quickly as you can.

Arranging

It's hard enough to summarize someone else's viewpoint in a sentence or two. But the challenge becomes even greater when you have to explain not just the principal claim but also the writer's reasons and the evidence. The big challenge to giving such a full summary is arrangement: How will you present the information? In what order will you put things? We can suggest two basic strategies: the play-by-play summary and the argument-breakdown summary. Both methods of summarizing begin with a brief description of the writer, the context, and the main idea (the principal argument).

Play-by-Play Summarizing: A play-by-play narrates each step in an argument. This can be done by summarizing each paragraph or by summarizing each major section (sometimes a paragraph, sometimes a whole chapter) in one or two sentences. The play-by-play summary shows how the argument progresses: What comes first? What comes second? What comes last? The play-by-play summary also guarantees that the summary will accurately present the order that the writer intended. Finally, the play-by-play summary catches all the major parts of the argument. Nothing significant will be left out.

Take this play-by-play summary of an opinion article, for instance:

Navarrette, Ruben. "Reformers Can't Ignore Illegal 'Criminal Aliens.'" *USA Today* 24 March 2010: 9A. Print.

In the heated debate about immigration reform, Ruben Navarrette notices that many "immigration foes…gladly latch on to the criminal-aliens issue." A syndicated columnist and San Diego resident, Navarrette admits that many illegal aliens commit crimes while in the United States. However, after pointing out some crime statistics, Navarrette insists that those supporting immigration reform should "confront this issue now." He says that allowing immigration opponents to make arguments about criminal illegal aliens will impede any kind of legislative reform. He next explains that illegal immigrants do not represent a disproportionate number of criminals in the United States. Navarrette then turns to history: "Since the beginnings of the Republic, nativists and others who oppose both legal and illegal immigration have tried to marginalize foreigners by painting them as somehow dangerous or detrimental. That is what was said about the Germans, Chinese, Jews, Irish and the Italians." Navarrette concludes by warning that if immigration proponents ignore the criminal illegal aliens, then they will "hurt the cause of millions of illegal immigrants who work hard, pay taxes and stay on the straight and narrow."

This brief example illustrates the strengths and the potential drawbacks of the play-by-play arrangement. After reading the summary, you have a clear sense of what the argument is and how it's presented. But you may not have a clear sense of what is most important. And some parts of the argument may seem out of place. For instance, Navarrette's digression to discuss American history seems like it does not follow from his discussion of illegal criminal aliens.

The Argument-Breakdown Summary: The argument-breakdown summary tries to take the argument apart and emphasize both its key components and their relation to one another. You point out, for example, the main claim and the key reasons supporting that claim without exactly repeating the argument's arrangement. Consider this summary of the same article:

Navarrette, Ruben. "Reformers Can't Ignore Illegal 'Criminal Aliens.' " *USA Today* 24 March 2010: 9A. Print.

In the heated debate about immigration reform, Ruben Navarrette argues that people who advocate for immigration reform cannot ignore the criminal illegal aliens in the United States. Navarrette concedes that many illegal aliens commit crimes, and he even offers some statistics to show that more than 80% of illegal aliens arrested by the Immigration and Custom Enforcement Agents of Los Angeles in December of 2010 had been convicted of crimes in the United States. Navarette worries that ignoring these criminal illegal aliens will harm efforts at immigration reform. He says, "those who commit crimes continue to hurt the cause of millions of illegal immigrants who work hard, pay taxes and stay on the straight and narrow. In that way, criminal aliens create a whole new crop of victims." Additionally, Navarrette says that ignoring criminal illegal aliens will allow people who oppose immigration reform to spread exaggerations and animosities. Since immigration opponents "gladly latch on to the criminal-aliens issue," immigration reformers "should address this head on." Navarrette offers two bits of evidence to show why immigration reformists must address the issue of illegal criminal aliens. First, he explains that illegal immigrants are not any more likely to be criminals than anyone else. And second, he reminds his audience of a disturbing historical trend that should not be repeated: "nativists and others who oppose both legal and illegal immigration have tried to marginalize foreigners by painting them as somehow dangerous or detrimental. That is what was said about the Germans, Chinese, Jews, Irish and the Italians." Navarrette concludes by saying that, if immigration reformers directly address the issue of criminal illegal aliens, then reformers can prevent such criminals from harming the rest of the law-abiding immigrant population.

As the above example demonstrates, sometimes an argument-breakdown summary will rearrange the parts of the argument. Navarrette, for instance, does not cleanly separate his two reasons. He doesn't say, "First we should deal with criminal illegal aliens in order to counter the impression that all illegal immigrants are criminals. And second, we should deal with criminal illegal aliens to keep those illegal immigrants who are criminal from poisoning the effort at immigration reform that will benefit the law-abiding immigrant community." But, in our summary, we separate the two reasons in order to demonstrate that they are equally important to his argument. The potential drawback of the argument-breakdown is that it may not be accurate or even fair to the source. By presenting someone else's ideas in a different order, we risk changing the ideas themselves. And by saying that a writer does something to accomplish a particular goal (like seeming fair or acknowledging the opposition), we speculate about motives that the editors may not have had in mind.

We encourage you to experiment a bit. Try writing both kinds of summary. Decide which suits your purpose best. Since there is no right way to summarize, you must pick the way that you feel is most helpful in mapping your controversy.

Documenting

You've likely noticed that every sample summary presented in this chapter (every sentence or paragraph summarizing another person's ideas) has included some kind of quote. You probably also noticed that the last two summaries featured the citation information for the *USA Today* article. This *citation information* allows you to find the source for yourself. Both the quotes and the citation information are methods of source documentation, showing the reader where the information came from.

In other classes, you've been asked to cite your sources, using parenthetical citations at the ends of sentences or footnotes or some other method. You've learned elaborate conventions for listing the page numbers or creating the works-cited pages. Maybe you wonder why you have to be so thorough with your documentation. Journalists don't list page numbers, compose endnotes, or include works-cited pages. Why not write like them? You can, if you're part of the journalistic community or writing to an audience that expects a certain level of evidence. As we will explain in this last segment, documentation conventions—like those in journalism—depend on: (1) the community's standards for documentation and (2) the audience's willingness to believe that a summary is fair and accurate. Before we give advice about how to document your sources, allow us to explain these two things. Knowing why you document your sources will help you to do so more effectively.

Community Standards: Communities worry about information in different ways. Journalists and audiences reading news media sources want current information that comes directly from the source. After finishing an article, readers don't want to hunt down the source themselves. So journalists don't have to give their audiences information about how to find the person or the report quoted in an article. But they have to explain to their audience who the person is or when the report was produced to show that this information is current. Academics (professors, students, researchers) want accurate information that they can consult themselves. They want to know where they can find a source. As a result, academic writers have to provide their audiences with more elaborate documentation. The journalist can simply introduce a quote by saying, "At a Tuesday press conference, Senator Warrington explained... ." The academic must introduce the quote and then provide a footnote or a works-cited page showing where she heard or read the Senator say such things. Your mapping-a-controversy essay will be written for an academic audience—for your instructor and your classmates. And since you're writing for an academic audience, you will have to follow the documentation conventions that show the audience where you got your information, down to the page number. We suggest the Modern Language Association (MLA) method of documentation, since it's the least elaborate of the documentation methods in the humanities and social sciences, and because it's clearly presented in your style guide.

The Audience's Willingness to Believe the Summary's Accuracy: Community standards for documentation are explicitly and carefully explained in style guides like the one you're using in this course. But the audience's willingness to believe is harder to figure out. People reading news media tend to be more willing to believe because they've learned to trust particular venues. If you read the *Wall Street Journal* every day, you likely believe that it's a reliable source and will trust the information presented in its many articles. Academics have learned to be skeptical. When you are writing to an audience who is more willing to believe, you can document less. But as the audience's skepticism grows, so does the need to document the source. Compare the following sentences, each offering more specific documentation of the source material:

No documentation—for an audience willing to accept the summary's accuracy: Internet-privacy activists believe that Facebook collects too much personal information in an unsecure database, thus putting all of its users at risk of identity theft and government spying.

Specific attribution—for a slightly skeptical audience: Internet-privacy alarmist Jeff Godwin believes that Facebook collects too much personal information in an unsecure database, thus putting all of its users at risk of identity theft and government spying.

Direct quote for a more skeptical audience: Internet-privacy activist Jeff Godwin says, "Facebook collects too much personal information in an unsecure database, thus putting all of its users at risk of identity theft and government spying."

Direct quote and source citation for a very skeptical audience: Internet-privacy activist Jeff Godwin writes on his blog GovernmentMindControlFactory. com (13 Jan. 2014), "Based on the recently released report from the Government

Accountability office, I believe that Facebook is hoarding too much data about our personal lives. Worse still, this information is kept in an unsecure database. We wouldn't have to worry so much about government spies or Internet identity thieves, if Facebook didn't make it so easy for them to get our information!"

You can imagine the audience responses that would prompt a writer to add the documentation information presented in each of the examples above. After reading the first example (without attribution), a skeptical reader might retort, "Really, I've never heard anyone say something so extreme." After the second (with attribution), a skeptical reader might respond, "I've read Godwin's recent book, and this doesn't sound like something he would say." After the third (with a direct quote), an even more skeptical reader might say, "I read that blog all the time and don't remember Godwin saying something so critical of Facebook. Where did you find this quote?" For this third reader, the direct quote with a source citation is necessary. Otherwise, our very skeptical audience member (the academic reader) will think we're unfairly or inaccurately summarizing Godwin's viewpoint.

Techniques for Documenting Sources in Academic Writing: Since you're writing to a skeptical (academic) audience, and since you're writing to a community that accepts certain standards for source citation (MLA), you will have to be very careful. Think of your efforts to document your sources not as a painful chore that you must complete because your instructor has required it. Documentation is not busy-work in a writing class. It's evidence to prove that your summary is fair and accurate. If you do not provide the appropriate kind and amount of evidence when summarizing a source, your reader will not trust or believe you.

So we suggest the following techniques in academic writing to show your audience that you are trustworthy:

1. Especially when summarizing without a direct quote, offer a citation (a parenthetical mention of the source): Austinites believe that the light rail system is a waste of money and should not be expanded beyond the one train line that Austin currently has (Cullen A23).
2. Qualify the attribution to specifically mention who believes these things: Some Austinites, such as City Councilwoman Marjorie Cullen, believe that the light rail system is a waste of money and should not be expanded beyond the one train line that Austin currently has (A23).
3. Provide a direct quote to show your reader that this is in fact what the stakeholder said: Some Austinites, such as City Councilwoman Marjorie Cullen, believe that the light rail system is a waste of money and should not be expanded beyond the one train line that Austin currently has. Cullen asks, "Why throw good money after bad?" Instead, she suggests, "Let's put more money into good roads" (A23).

4. Provide a source citation that will show your reader where to find the source: Some Austinites, such as City Councilwoman Marjorie Cullen, believe that the light rail system is a waste of money and should not be expanded beyond the one train line that Austin currently has. Cullen asks, "Why throw good money after bad?" Instead, she suggests, "Let's put more money into good roads" (A23).

Work Cited

Cullen, Marjorie. "Light Rail a Boondoggle." *Austin Independent* 14 Feb. 2012. Web.

The above techniques will assure your skeptical academic audience that your summary is indeed fair and accurate. As an added bonus, these techniques will show your instructor that you have done your research and that you are not plagiarizing (copying) another person's work without citation. Plagiarism is a serious academic concern because, when students copy other people's writing, they do not learn to write themselves. If you always attribute quotes to the people who originally wrote or said these things, if you always cite your sources, and if you always show your instructors when you are directly quoting someone, you will look like a trustworthy source and a good student.

How Much to Quote: After you've documented your source, you will still have two more things to worry about: how much to quote and how to introduce the quote. Consult your handbook to learn the mechanical differences among different methods of quoting: a brief quote that selects a word or two, a full-sentence quote, and a block quote. Here, we offer examples of each and some advice about when to use them:

1. *Brief Quote:* Some Austinites, such as City Councilwoman Marjorie Cullen, believe that the light rail system is a waste of money and should not be expanded beyond the one train line that Austin currently has. She suggests putting "more money into good roads" (Cullen A23).
2. *Full Sentence Quote:* Some Austinites, such as City Councilwoman Marjorie Cullen, believe that the light rail system is a waste of money and should not be expanded beyond the one train line that Austin currently has. Cullen asks, "Why throw good money after bad? Let's get off this crazy train. Let's put more money into good roads" (A23).
3. *Block Quote:* Some Austinites, such as City Councilwoman Marjorie Cullen, believe that the light rail system is a waste of money and should not be expanded beyond the one train line that Austin currently has. Cullen asks,

   Why throw good money after bad? Let's get off this crazy train. Let's put more money into good roads. Roads—even toll roads—get people in outlying communities, such as Manor and Kyle, into the city. Roads will actually be used by Central Texas residents. I don't know if you've been on the train lately, but, when I see it drive by, it's always empty. And, finally, roads will allow Austin to grow the way citizens want. Train lines force urban growth where the train stations happen to be located. (A23)

Your decision about how much to quote should be guided by two questions: How much information do you want to provide about the source? And how much is your reader likely to question your summary's accuracy? If you want to really capture the full content and the color of a writer's prose, then the block quote is the way to go. If you're writing to an audience who will skeptically interrogate your summary, then the block quote is preferred. If, on the other hand, you're writing to a less skeptical audience, and you just want to get the basic message across, the brief quote will suffice.

How to Introduce a Quote: Earlier in this chapter, under the heading "Contextualizing," we talked about introducing the speaker and the context to help your reader understand what's at stake in a viewpoint. Here, when we mention "how to introduce a quote," we mean something much more specific: the verbs and adverbs of attribution. These are the words that tell your reader how someone expresses himself. The block quote, mentioned above, does a good job of capturing the writer's tone, but the block quote also requires you to reproduce a large chunk of writing. Using verbs and adverbs of attribution, you can convey tone without repeating so much of another person's prose. The most common verb of attribution is *say*: Johnson says, "Toll roads are nothing but a way for developers to make money." The verb of attribution allows you to present a source's *tone*, how the writer says what he says. Other words can help you to accomplish this as well. Adverbs—such as *sarcastically*, *indignantly*, or *calmly*—can convey tone. You should use such words to show your reader the writer's tone, but be fair. Certain adverbs and verbs of attribution will make a source seem less trustworthy. There's a big difference between "Johnson petulantly retorts" and "Johnson disagrees." The writer who uses phrasing like "petulantly retorts" seems less credible because he is less objective.

CHAPTER

3 | Mapping the Controversy

A fter finding and summarizing some viewpoints, you're ready to start mapping the controversy. In this chapter, we will discuss strategies for making sense of all the information that you've collected.

Before we get into the specific strategies, we want to make a general point about mapping the controversy. As you can probably imagine, a series of summaries presented one after another can be confusing and a little boring: John wants to ban capital punishment in Texas; Mary wants to permit lethal injections but with a new drug combination; and Eddy wants to keep the death penalty exactly as it is. To make the controversy interesting and to give your reader a clear view of the big picture, you must *synthesize* the information. Explain what is most important. Demonstrate the key points in the controversy. Show your reader how everything fits together.

In this chapter, we offer a few strategies for synthesis. Each strategy focuses on an aspect of the controversy. By focusing on an aspect of the controversy, each strategy says to the reader, "This is most important!" We encourage you to choose the strategy—or strategies—that allow you to emphasize what you think is most important about your controversy. You should, of course, represent a ll viewpoints fairly. Don't take a side in the controversy. But do tell your readers what aspects of the controversy deserve their attention.

Focusing on the Stakeholders

Since you have found viewpoint articles, the most obvious way to synthesize your material is by focusing on stakeholders. In your summaries of selected viewpoint articles, introduce one stakeholder, explain his/her interests, summarize his/her viewpoint, and relate that viewpoint to the others. Not only is this the most obvious strategy, but it also may be the most effective. Maybe the controversy makes sense when seen as a series of arguments put forward by people with different interests. And maybe focusing on the stakeholders shows your reader the connections between these people's interests and their viewpoints. No other strategy, for example, will more clearly show us that petroleum-industry executives favor hydrofracking because their companies stand to make a lot of money from this drilling technique. Or that environmentalists oppose hydrofracking because they fear it will damage the local ecosystem, which they value deeply.

Nonetheless, focusing on the stakeholders may have a few drawbacks as well. To begin with, explaining each stakeholder and his/her viewpoint separately will make it difficult for you to relate the viewpoints to one another. Are environmentalists responding to corporate executives' arguments?

Furthermore, focusing on the stakeholders may overlook the most interesting thing about a controversy. Often, stakeholders have different interests but arrive at the same position. If you focus on the stakeholders, then you may end up with a series of summaries that seem to say the same thing with only a few subtle differences: Politicians who want to please their constituents favor tax reform; voters who want to lower taxes favor tax reform; corporate executives who want to simplify their accounting practices favor tax reform. The points of agreement are not terribly interesting, though they are important. We should note that politicians, voters, and corporate executives all favor tax reform. But in order to really understand this controversy, we need to focus on the viewpoints themselves.

Focusing on the Viewpoints

Maybe you don't want to focus on the stakeholders. Maybe you're more interested in discussing the places where they agree and disagree. If one viewpoint brings together several stakeholders—"everyone favors tax reform"—then you may want to begin your summary of a particular source by pointing out the common belief. Then you can summarize this source's viewpoint. Finally, you can explain how this particular source differs from others:

> Many people oppose hydrofracking because they fear it will damage the environment. Environmentalists, for instance, worry about pollution, which could hurt local wildlife. Some environmentalists also worry about releasing methane gas, which, they argue, contributes to global warming. The environmentalist's concerns are similar to those held by local residents. But, instead of worrying about widespread damage to wildlife and global climate, local residents worry that hydrofracking will cause earthquakes in their backyards and pollute their water supply.

Above we have a summary of the viewpoint held by environmentalists—one group of stakeholders. The summary opens by mentioning a belief that environmentalists share with other stakeholders. And the summary ends by comparing the environmentalists' concerns with those of local residents. In this case, focusing on the viewpoints has allowed us to emphasize the different reasons behind a seemingly common position. Environmentalists have one set of reasons (damage to wildlife and global climate), while local residents have another set of reasons (harm to property and quality of life).

Focusing on the viewpoints also allows you to compare the points of agreement and disagreement in a controversy. If you want to explain how these viewpoints relate to one another, you can demonstrate that people share some beliefs, but they nonetheless disagree about a few key things. For example:

> Everyone agrees that hydrofracking deserves to be studied so that we can closely monitor its impact on the environment. Jim Jeffries, a petroleum engineer who works for OilCo, says, "We are learning new things every day, and we need to reevaluate this technology constantly to make sure we get the most out of our natural resources without harming the environment." Jeffries agrees with others, such as Lana Eggerstrom of the Environmental Advocacy Organization. Eggerstrom explains, "Hydrofracking is no different from nuclear power—it has lots of potential but many dangers, so we need to be very careful and watchful, or we will hurt the planet and ourselves." Unlike Eggerstrom, who believes that the government should regulate hydrofracking, Jeffries believes that the industry should monitor itself.

In the above example, we focus on the viewpoints, so we can highlight key areas of agreement and disagreement in the debate. By highlighting the agreements and disagreements, we can show how these viewpoints fit together.

Before moving on to the next strategy for synthesis, we want to emphasize that you don't have to choose one strategy or another. You may decide, initially, to focus on one particularly important stakeholder. Afterwards, you may focus the remainder of your summary on the viewpoint to show that there are many other perspectives relating to this viewpoint in different ways. For example:

> In the debate about what to do with the vacant shopping mall near Interstate 12, one stakeholder strongly favors replacing the property with high-rise luxury apartments. Developer and real-estate mogul Henry Kastings claims that, if he were allowed to build apartments, then the city would benefit while he profits. Many oppose Kastings but for different reasons. They all agree that a high-rise apartment complex would not benefit the city, though it might enrich Mr. Kastings. They suggest alternate uses for the property. Some community residents suggest that the city convert the space into a public amphitheater. Some advocates for the poor want to replace the vacant mall with low-income housing. Kastings takes these differing viewpoints into account by explaining that the city cannot afford to build a public amphitheater. But, he notes, the city could increase revenue by collecting property taxes from luxury-apartment residents. Kastings further explains that the I-12 shopping mall is in a poor location for low-income housing because it is far from public transportation. Luxury apartment residents, he explains, do not rely on the bus system. Since they tend to drive their own cars, such wealthy residents may prefer to be near the Interstate because they would have ready access to a major roadway.

The sample paragraphs that we provide in this section suggest strategies for synthesis, but the work remains incomplete. A fuller controversy map would include numerous summaries that present the relevant viewpoints, while drawing connections among these viewpoints. Below, we offer one more strategy for synthesizing the information about a controversy.

Focusing on the Questions

Each of the strategies presented in this chapter has advantages and disadvantages. And each strategy is appropriate to certain circumstances. Before getting into the final strategy, let's review:

Strategy	Advantages	Disadvantages	When the Strategy Is Appropriate
Focusing on Stakeholders	Emphasizes the connections among people's interests, knowledge, and values and their viewpoints	Makes comparison among viewpoints difficult	When the stakeholders do not share claims or reasons
Focusing on Viewpoints	Allows comparison of agreements and disagreements among stakeholders	De-emphasizes stakeholders	When some stakeholders share common ground (a common viewpoint or common reasons) but disagree nonetheless
Focusing on Questions	Allows emphasis on the key questions that people are debating	De-emphasizes stakeholders and makes comparison among viewpoints difficult	When one or two key questions dominate the debate or when people seem to be talking past one another

As the above table demonstrates, focusing on the questions has notable advantages and disadvantages. This strategy is appropriate in certain circumstances. Before learning about the strategy itself, let's take a moment to think about the circumstances in which it is appropriate to focus on the questions.

One or Two Questions Dominate the Debate: When we argue, we frequently return to one or two (often related) questions. Our argument will confuse an uninformed eavesdropper, unless someone can clearly explain what central questions we are debating. Such questions are often important, though they remain unstated. Consider the debate about capital punishment. People argue about a central question: Should the United States execute criminals? This very simple question h as produced a very complicated discussion. That's because this simple question relates to three other questions, which typically remain unstated: (1) Does capital punishment deter crime? (2) Is capital punishment justly administered? (3) Is the death penalty a form of cruel and unusual punishment? If you answer "yes" to questions 1 and 2 and "no" to question 3—"Capital punishment deters crime, is justly administered, and is neither cruel nor unusual"—then you likely support capital punishment. And, conversely, if you answer "no" to questions 1 and 2 but "yes" to question 3—"Capital punishment does not deter crime, is not justly administered, and is both cruel and unusual"—then you likely oppose the death penalty.

But, what if you think the death penalty is a just punishment that deters crime, but you also worry that too many innocent people get executed because of flaws in our criminal justice system? Or you think that capital punishment is justly administered, and you think it deters crime, but you believe that the current manner of executing people (lethal injection) is cruel and unusual? In either case, you won't support or oppose capital punishment. You will favor reform—keeping but improving capital punishment. In this case—and in many others—if you want to understand the controversy, you really need to understand the questions. If you fail to understand the questions, you may end up believing that there are two sides: for and against the death penalty. But if you understand the questions, then you can see that there are many sides. There are some who support and some who oppose capital punishment. But there are many others. Some want to have a moratorium (a period when we don't execute criminals) so that we can fix the justice system. Some want to find a more humane way to administer the punishment. When you have such a complicated debate, often the best way to make sense of things is to state explicitly the main questions and their relations to one another.

When People Seem To Be Talking Past One Another: Certainly you've participated in or witnessed disagreements when people did not seem to acknowledge or even understand each other. They seem to be talking to someone else but not to the person in the room. This often happens because people argue about completely different questions. In order for a debate to go anywhere—in order for people to work toward any kind of agreement—participants must first agree to argue about the same thing. If we disagree about the question, we will never agree about the answer to the question. Take two classic debates in American culture today, abortion and gun control. In both cases, many of the disputants do not agree about the basic question at issue. For the pro-lifer the question at issue is, "Does life begin at conception?" For the pro-choicer the question is, "Does a woman's right to privacy include her right to an abortion?" For the gun-control advocate the question is, "Do guns, made readily available to the public, endanger people's safety and security?" For the gun-rights advocate the question is, "Do gun-control laws violate the Second Constitutional Amendment?" If you can show these differing questions to your reader, then you can explain why the debates have lasted so long and why it's so hard to get people to find any points of agreement.

Some Terms to Help You Identify Questions: Needless to say, people argue over an endless variety of questions. We can never classify them all. But we can use stasis theory, a simple guide that's been around in one form or another since the Ancient Greeks. The basic idea behind stasis theory is that people tend to argue about certain kinds of questions.

- **Questions of fact:** What exists? What has existed? What is likely to exist?
- **Questions of cause and effect:** What causes lead to what effects? What effects tend to come from what causes?
- **Questions of definition:** What do we call something? In what category does something belong?

- **Questions of value:** Is something good or bad? Just or unjust? Beautiful or ugly?
- **Questions of procedure:** What should we do?

According to classical stasis theory, people tend to disagree first about questions of fact, next about cause and effect, then definition, value, and finally procedure. This is often illustrated with a murder trial:

> First, we disagree about the facts of the matter: Did John stab Edward? If we can finally agree about the facts (yes, John did stab Edward), then we may still disagree about the cause: Did John stab Edward because Edward was attacking John or because John was angry with Edward? If we agree about the cause (John stabbed Edward because he was angry with Edward), we may disagree about what to call the act: Is this premeditated murder, or is it an accidental killing? And if we agree about what to call it—this is premeditated murder—we may still disagree about the value: Is this an unforgivable crime or a terrible but nonetheless understandable offense? Lastly, even if we agree to call this an unforgivable crime, we may still disagree about what to do: Should we put John in jail for 30 years or 10 years?

The murder trial is a helpful example, but it doesn't seem to apply to public arguments. So let's apply stasis theory to a current public controversy:

- **Questions of Fact:** Is the earth getting warmer? Are global climate patterns changing?
- **Questions of Cause and Effect:** Is human activity the main cause behind these changes to global climate patterns? Do greenhouse gases principally resulting from human activity lead to global warming?
- **Questions of Definition:** Is this "global warming"? Is it "global climate change"? Is it "global weirding"? Is it a "media hoax"?
- **Questions of Value:** Is global warming, even if caused by humans, all that bad? Is economic growth more important than protecting the environment?
- **Questions of Procedure:** Should developing nations have to reduce their carbon emissions as much as industrialized nations? Would a "cap-and-trade" system work better or worse than strict limits on carbon emissions?

At the moment, we are debating all of these questions. But some questions are more important than others, so they get more attention in a debate about "global climate change." If you were mapping this controversy, your job would be to show your reader which questions—fact, cause and effect, definition, value, or procedure—are most important. Which receive the most attention in the debate?

You can use stasis theory to highlight the most important question(s) in a controversy. For instance, you might argue: "Though people are debating many questions in the controversy about global climate change, the biggest and most important question is about fact: Is the earth getting warmer?" Or you might say:

Among those who accept that the earth is getting warmer due to human activity, there is still a debate about procedure: How can we stop or at least slow down global climate change? Suresh Swaminathan, an economist for the RAND Corporation, believes that radical proposals to dramatically reduce global carbon emissions will have dire economic consequences. Since he values economic growth, Swaminathan recommends that governments invest in technological development to promote alternatives to coal and oil in transportation and power.

Regardless of the strategy you choose, your goal is to give your reader a sense of the overall debate. To do that, you will have to synthesize the information. Summarize the viewpoints. While summarizing these viewpoints, also map the controversy. Show how the viewpoints relate to one another, and how they fit together into a larger debate.

CHAPTER 4

Rhetorical Analysis, An Introduction

I n your next major essay, you will analyze an argument that has contributed to your chosen controversy. Before guiding you through the steps of rhetorical analysis, we want to begin this chapter with a quick definition.

A *rhetorical analysis* is any effort to explain persuasion with reference to audience and situation. You've already written one kind of rhetorical analysis. While mapping your controversy, you explained a series of arguments with reference to the audience (the stakeholders) and the situation (the stakeholders' interests, the controversy's history, the community's values and beliefs). In this unit, you will write another kind of rhetorical analysis. Instead of focusing on a controversy, you'll focus on one text—one article, one interview, one video or image. Instead of explaining how several viewpoints fit together in a conversation, you'll explain how the reasons and the evidence fit together in an argument. Instead of showing how the viewpoints move the controversy in one direction or another, you'll show how the reasons and the evidence move the audience to believe one thing or another.

While some of your professors write rhetorical analyses simply for the fun of it, you have written and will write rhetorical analyses to prepare you for writing a persuasive argument. Rhetorical analysis is *strategic*. It helps people understand the situation and the audience in order to be more persuasive. After mapping a controversy and analyzing an argument, you'll be well prepared to persuade an audience.

There's another way to think about rhetorical analysis, something to keep in mind as you strategize. Rhetorical analysis is *ethical*. Rhetorical analysis teaches us to be more considerate of those with whom we disagree. And rhetorical analysis teaches us to be critical of those with whom we agree.

To analyze an argument that doesn't persuade you, you must take the reasons seriously. And you must think carefully about why those reasons would move a group of reasonable people. So the first step in rhetorical analysis involves putting aside your own beliefs. Your question is not, "Do I find this argument convincing?" but instead, "Why would these people find this argument convincing?" Since your aim is to answer this second question, you cannot dismiss the audience or the argument as simply "wrong" or "wrong-headed." Even though you may not agree, you do have to listen carefully. Listening to one another carefully and considerately prevents our controversies from turning into wars.

If you're analyzing an argument that persuades you, then you have already listened carefully and considerately. In this case, rhetorical analysis will help you to listen critically. Your question now becomes, "How does this argument persuade someone like me?" Once you see that your own beliefs are based on someone else's persuasive efforts, you may feel a little less committed to that viewpoint. Just like people you disagree with, you base your beliefs on persuasive arguments. And just as the considerate person won't go to war with someone he understands, the critical person won't go to war over something she questions. Being critical doesn't mean you have to give up on your beliefs, nor does being considerate mean that you have to change your mind. You can remain committed while listening considerately and believing critically. When you are critical, considerate, and nonetheless still committed, you will keep arguing. Since arguing with words is preferable to fighting with weapons, rhetorical analysis is good for us.

The Basics of Rhetorical Analysis: Speaker, Audience, Situation, Text

Any sort of analysis requires that you take something apart. Analysis begins with disassembling and labeling. The next three chapters introduce you to techniques for doing that. In order to teach you how to disassemble an argument and label its parts, we will define the parts of an argument and we will tell you how to find those parts. (On your RHE 306 Canvas site, you can find sample analyses to complement the chapters to follow.) The four major parts that you must identify and label in any rhetorical analysis are the speaker, the audience, the situation, and the text.

The Speaker: The speaker is the person, the organization, or the company trying to persuade. Sometimes it's difficult to pinpoint exactly who the speaker is. Corporate advertisements, for instance, are often produced by marketing firms, even though they speak for the companies they represent. Is Nike or Wieden+Kennedy telling you to "Just do it"? It's often easiest and best simply to assume that the speaker is the person or the group identified in the argument: Whoever is presented as the speaker is the speaker. In a Nike advertisement, therefore, the Nike corporation is the speaker. An introductory-level rhetorical analysis, such as the one you must write, can settle on the *ostensible speaker* (the person or organization who seems to be trying to persuade). But a more sophisticated rhetorical analysis might distinguish between the *ostensible speaker*, the *real speaker*, and the *implied speaker*. To return to our earlier example, the ostensible speaker in a Nike shoe commercial is Nike. The real speaker is the advertising firm (Wieden+Kennedy). The implied speaker is the star of the commercial, the athlete who runs up a flight of stairs and breathlessly declares, "Just do it!"

For the time being, we encourage you to focus on the ostensible speaker—the person or organization presented in the text as the persuader. Hereafter, we will simply use the term "speaker." And we suggest that you divide your knowledge about this speaker into two categories: invented and situated. There is the information you learn about the speaker from the text itself. This is *invented* information because the speaker presents it in the body of her argument. Speakers use invented information to present themselves in the best possible light. For example, the speaker may reveal that she knows a lot by citing expert sources; she may reveal that she is part of a community by referencing insider information; she may show that she cares about certain things by saying, "Like you, I value education and family." On the other hand, there is information that the audience is likely to know about the speaker before reading the argument. This is *situated* information because it is established before the speaker begins to persuade. You can find situated information about the speaker by looking for articles about the person's or the organization's reputation. Other arguments by this speaker can also teach you about this person's or this organization's reputation.

The Audience: In Chapter 1, when we were discussing stakeholders—their beliefs, values, and interests—we presented some basic terms that explain who an audience is and why they might care about an issue. These same terms can explain why people might find certain reasons persuasive. For instance, an audience that values the environment is more likely to be persuaded by an argument against hydrofracking that points to environmental damage. An audience interested in keeping health insurance costs low is likely to be interested in—that is, persuaded by—a plan that promises to reduce premiums. And an audience that believes violent crime is not associated with personal consumption of marijuana is more likely to accept the assertion that legalizing cannabis will not lead to a spike in crime.

Research, as we explain above, can teach you about the speaker; it can also teach you about the audience: their beliefs, values, and interests. Particularly, you can look at two types of sources: (1) direct feedback from the audience and (2) other arguments written to this audience. If members of the audience respond to an argument by saying, "yes, we agree," then you can look at their reasons for agreeing. Imagine, for example, that a newspaper editorial tries to convince a group of Illinois residents that they should not vote for a candidate for the U.S. Senate because that candidate doesn't live in Illinois. She's a "carpetbagger"—someone who opportunistically moves to an area to win an election. Such argument presumes that the audience values home-state residence. Imagine, also, that many voters write letters to the editor to say, "We don't care about where she lives. We only care that she represents our beliefs in the U.S. Senate." The audience's response indicates that, instead of valuing a candidate's residency, they value the candidate's positions. As a result, they are not persuaded. There is strategic value to understanding why this audience is not persuaded. The speaker could, for example, rework the argument to appeal to the audience's values: "Since she doesn't live in Illinois, she won't consistently understand what the community wants, and eventually, her positions will not reflect what is best for our state. Right now she may say things that we like, but later she will not."

Another way to learn about an audience's values, interests, and knowledge, is to look at other arguments published in the same venue. If you're reading an article published in the *Austin American-Statesman*, you can assume that this newspaper's audience shares its political bias. By reading editorials published in this newspaper, you can figure out whether the audience is liberal, conservative, or moderate. You can figure out what concerns these people. You can determine what they know (since they learn from the articles in the newspaper).

The Situation: An effective argument must speak to *history* and to *exigency*. These two factors constitute what we call the *situation*. For instance, if you want to build an argument against providing federal disaster relief to victims of tornadoes in the Midwest, you will have to consider the past efforts to provide federal disaster relief to hurricane victims on the East Coast and the Gulf Coast. Your audience will likely know this *history*, so they will expect you to discuss it: Why provide federal support

Further Discussion: On your RHE 306 Canvas site, you can find several articles about this year's common topic. Pick one of these articles. Read it. Summarize the argument, and describe the audience by completing the following templates:

- This article assumes that the audience already believes _____. This is evident when the editors say, "_____."
- This article assumes that the audience already values _____. This is evident when the editors mention _____.
- This article assumes that the audience shares an interest in _____. This is evident where the editors discuss _____.

When you complete these sentences, you will have a fair description of the *intended* audience for this argument—the people whom the speaker is trying to convince. But intended audiences often fail to match up with *real* audiences, the people who actually read an argument. You can learn about the intended audience by looking at the text itself. You can learn about the *real* audience by looking outside the text. We suggest two sources:

1. The comments posted by *actual* readers. Online sources often include comments in the footer, below the article. Print sources often solicit responses that appear in other print formats. Letters to the editor, for example, are short pieces written by readers in response to specific articles.

2. Other opinion articles on similar subjects found in the same venue.

Using the information you find in the readers' comments answer these questions: What do you think a specific reader believes or values? What are his expressed interests? Based on your research into other articles, what do you think the typical reader of this magazine, newspaper, or website believes or values? What is she interested in? Finally, do the beliefs, values, and interests identified as belonging to this article's intended audience match those of its real audience?

for hurricane relief but not for tornado relief? Another component of history is the *exigency*, the immediate event or argument that has prompted someone to speak or write. It may be a recent event (a tornado that destroyed a town in Oklahoma). It may be a recent argument (a governor's public demand that the president declare this town a federal disaster area). That exigency might combine with history. People's experience of a recent tornado might combine with their knowledge of past tornadoes and their memory of federal money previously spent rebuilding in tornado-prone areas. This combination of recent events and past experience might prompt the community to debate federal disaster relief for the area. The history and the exigency, like the audience, can be researched.

The Text: So far, we have used the term "text" to reference the thing you will analyze. On your RHE 306 Canvas site, you can find an analysis of a text, using the vocabulary introduced in this chapter. We would like to stress, however, that "text" can refer to any argument. Rhetorical analysis applies to anything intended to persuade: a printed editorial, a graphic image, a video commercial, a movie, an item of clothing, a speech. The first question to ask when analyzing any text is: Does the speaker make this argument implicitly or explicitly? We introduced the terms "implicit" and "explicit" in Chapter 2, but here's a quick refresher. An explicit claim is stated openly. The speaker tells you to believe, feel, or do something. An implicit claim is suggested. The speaker tells you many things, and you arrive at the conclusion that the speaker wants you to accept.

This distinction between "implicit" and "explicit" points to the first key rhetorical element in any text—the *claim*. The claim is the principal idea that the audience should accept after encountering an argument. Claims come in many shapes and sizes. We suggest you think of claims in three ways. Some claims encourage the audience to *believe*. Some claims ask the audience to *feel*. And some claims petition the audience to *act*. When you are analyzing an implicit claim, you must state it in your own words since the speaker does not state it directly. You can use the following templates to guide you:

- The argument tells the audience to believe that _____.
- The argument encourages the audience to feel _____.
- The argument enjoins the audience to do _____.

> **Further Discussion:** So far, we have discussed three topics of research that will inform a rhetorical analysis—you can learn about the speaker, the audience, and the situation. All this information will help you to explain why the speaker chooses to make certain appeals. On your RHE 306 Canvas site, you will find a sample student paper—a research summary of a supplementary text—that was completed while the student was writing a rhetorical analysis of a separate argument. What does this research summary teach you about the speaker, the audience, and/or the situation?

If you are analyzing an explicit argument, the claim will be stated somewhere in the text. You can simply quote it. Here are a few rules of thumb that will help you to separate implicit from explicit claims:

- Arguments made in political and legal forums (opinion pages in the newspaper, congressional hearings, TV talk shows, courtrooms, corporate boardroom meetings) tend to be explicit.
- Arguments made in forums that aim to inform or entertain (documentary films, TV advertisements, movies, images, popular songs) tend to be implicit.
- Arguments that call for action tend to be explicit.
- Arguments that encourage feeling tend to be implicit.
- Arguments made to audiences who are inclined to agree with the speaker tend to be explicit.
- Arguments made to audiences who are inclined to disagree with the speaker tend to be implicit.

Everything in the text apart from the claim either supports or undermines the claim. The speaker wants to move the audience to believe, feel, or do something. So he or she gives *reasons* to support the claim. As you will learn in the next chapter, anything can be a reason. In a speech, a calm tone of voice can ask you to trust the speaker, and this trust can lead you to believe what the speaker says. In a movie, the music can make you tense, so you become more susceptible to being frightened. *Reasons*, as we'll explain in Chapter 5, are things that the speaker makes up. *Evidence*, on the other hand, is the stuff the speaker finds. If a speaker wants to make you feel disgusted by the amount of trash that U.S. residents produce, she might, for example, show you the Pacific garbage patch. She didn't make up the garbage patch. She found it. She might use especially moving language to describe the garbage patch: "gross," "horrendous," "oozing." This language

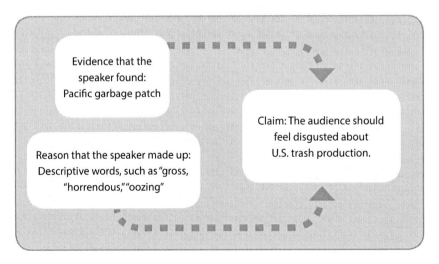

Evidence that the speaker found: Pacific garbage patch

Reason that the speaker made up: Descriptive words, such as "gross," "horrendous," "oozing"

Claim: The audience should feel disgusted about U.S. trash production.

is a reason, one she creates or makes up, to further the claim: You should feel disgusted about how much trash U.S. residents produce.

As shown above, the reason and the evidence work together to convince the audience that they should feel a certain way. In the next two chapters, we will talk in much greater detail about reasons and evidence. For now, as you initially consider the text you want to analyze, we encourage you to separate the claim from the rest of the material in the argument. If you can, try to classify anything that's not a claim as a "reason" or as "evidence."

Brief Exercise: Below, we offer a table that categorizes the kinds of evidence (both textual and contextual) that you can find to inform your analysis of the speaker, the audience, and the situation. We also offer suggestions for where to look to find such evidence.

	Textual Evidence	Contextual Evidence
Speaker	Invented information about the speaker: moments in the text when the speaker identifies his or her qualities, interests, or knowledge; aspects of the text (e.g., writing style, citations) that tell you about the speaker's qualities, interests, or knowledge	Situated information about the speaker: biographical information that the audience is likely to know when they recognize the speaker. This can be found by looking at articles about the speaker or other persuasive efforts composed by the speaker.
Audience	Information about the intended audience: The values, interests, and beliefs that the argument appeals to all belong to the intended audience	Information about the real audience: The values, interests, and beliefs that belong to real people who encounter this argument. Gather this information by looking at readers' responses to the argument and by looking at other arguments that the real audience finds persuasive.
Situation	Information about the situation that is mentioned in the argument itself	Information about the situation that can be learned by finding other sources

Once you've selected the text you want to analyze, try to find one bit of textual evidence to fit in each of the boxes in the "Textual Evidence" column. Try to find a quote, paragraph, or phrase that demonstrates invented information about the speaker, a description of the intended audience, or a description of the situation. Then try to find secondary texts with information to fill in the boxes in the "Contextual Evidence" column, such as an article, encyclopedia entry, or web page that demonstrates situated information about the speaker, information about the real audience, or information about the situation that is not mentioned directly in the text.

CHAPTER 5 | Reasons That People Invent

Arguments happen in places—at parties, in magazines, on websites. And the places matter a lot. One argument will be very well received in one place but not in another. Your friends will likely agree when you say that a professor should move an exam date so that you can go home early for spring break. On the other hand, saying the same thing to the professor would not persuade. In the previous chapter, we offered tools for analyzing context, the places where arguments happen. Context is the most important rhetorical element because the best argument in the worst place or at the wrong time will fail miserably.

The next two chapters offer tools for analyzing the text—the parts of an argument and their relation to one another. This chapter will focus on *reasons*, and the next chapter will discuss *evidence*. Both reasons and evidence encourage an audience to believe a claim. Speakers invent or make up reasons. Speakers find or research evidence. When we say that reasons are *invented*, we don't mean that they are fictitious or false. We mean that reasons come from creativity. Evidence comes from research. Speakers generally find their reasons first. When trying to think of ways to appeal to an audience, ask yourself, "How can I get these people to trust me? To feel a certain way? To do something?" The answers to these questions lead you to possible reasons. If the reasons by themselves are not convincing, then you may need to find evidence that will further support your reasons.

To illustrate, let's go back to our earlier example: trying to convince a professor to delay the mid-term exam so you can go home early for spring break. For this audience (the professor) in this situation (the classroom), your argument is not convincing. So you need to think of some good reasons. You brainstorm for a little while. Here's what you invent:

1. Delaying the exam will let you (the professor) go home early too.
2. Delaying the exam will make the class like you (the professor).
3. Delaying the exam will let us (the students) study over spring break, so we (students) will be better prepared for the final.
4. Delaying the exam will let us (the students) spend valuable time with our families.

You decide that the third reason is most likely to convince your professor because you've heard her explain that she cares about student performance.

So you go to class, and you state your claim followed by your reason. When she hears your argument, your professor chuckles a bit and responds, "You won't study over spring break; you'll forget a lot of what you've learned; and you'll do even worse on the mid-term." Undaunted, you decide that you will find some evidence to support your reason. How about a survey? You ask all the students in the class if they studied over Thanksgiving break. Seventy-two percent (72%) report that they did. Or maybe you find some examples from previous classes. Last fall, three biology seminars had tests right before Thanksgiving break, and two had tests right after. You learn that students in the seminars with exams after Thanksgiving break earned much higher grades than students with exams before Thanksgiving break. Of course, we're just making up this evidence as an example. It may be entirely false, and false evidence will make an argument embarrassingly unconvincing. Liars invent evidence. Convincing speakers invent reasons; then they find evidence.

Sometimes, reasons do not require evidence. You don't need to prove to your professor that letting students take the exam after spring break will allow her to leave town a day early. We will discuss the relationship between reasons and evidence more fully in the next chapter. For now, we encourage you to make this distinction: Speakers invent reasons, but they find evidence. And we encourage you to notice that evidence is typically—but not always—introduced to support reasons.

Like many guides to rhetoric and argumentation—some over 2,000 years old—we divide reasons into three categories: reasons to trust the speaker; reasons to feel a certain way; reasons to believe a certain thing. An effective argument will offer some combination of all three. Next, we define each type of reason, and we explain how it contributes to an argument's efficacy. On your RHE 306 Canvas site, you can find a sample analysis that demonstrates how these reasons come together in a real argument that is relevant to this year's topic.

Reasons to Trust

The first thing that a speaker must do is to win the audience's trust. If you don't trust someone, you won't believe what he says, no matter how well researched, persuasive, or moving the message might be. In fact, a persuasive argument coming from someone you don't trust is likely to be doubly rejected. You might think that such an untrustworthy person has persuaded you by lying and manipulating your emotions. If you do trust someone, on the other hand, then you will be more likely to feel what she asks you to feel and to believe what she asks you to believe.

In the previous chapter, we discussed two types of information that you can learn about the speaker: invented information and situated information. The *situated* information is the evidence—the information that the audience already knows about the speaker. Knowing that someone is a research scientist, a university professor, an award-winning journalist, or a famous inventor will make an audience more inclined to trust what she says. But there are other *invented* reasons to trust a speaker. Even if we don't know a person's expertise beforehand, we can pay close attention to the information that he presents. If he offers plenty of factual information, cites authorities, and seems to know the subject, then we have good reason to trust him just as we would an expert authority. A speaker who has both the situated and the invented expertise—a renowned research scientist who speaks authoritatively—will surely gain the audience's trust.

When you are looking for the textual elements that earn an audience's trust, we encourage you to find the situated information about the speaker, but we also encourage you to look for the invented reasons. Within the text, a speaker can show that she is smart and well informed by demonstrating two things: knowledge of the subject and an ability to respond appropriately to the situation.

Knowledge of the subject: Someone who shows you that she's learned a lot of information about a subject is someone you will likely trust as an authority even if she doesn't have the credentials.

An ability to respond appropriately to the situation: A writer's style shows you that he is smart enough to speak appropriately to the situation. An egghead speaks formally at a party, and a dolt uses slang in a college essay. The truly savvy person knows when to speak in what manner. In this textbook, we've made conscious decisions about our style to show that we understand the classroom situation. Since we're writing to students, we have chosen to write in a somewhat informal style. We use first- and second-person pronouns (*we, you*); we use contractions (*don't, isn't*); we throw in the occasional sentence fragment ("How about a survey?"). We do all of this to appear friendly. If we wanted to write more formally, then we might have written, "It is more likely that a highly formalized style will persuade an audience of first-year writing (FYW) students better than a colloquial lexicon or a paratactic syntax." This formal sentence might convince you that we are authorities. Who else but qualified writing teachers would know what a "paratactic syntax" is? But the authoritative style is less appropriate to the classroom situation because it will not help you to learn the material.

Knowledge of the subject and appropriateness of the writing style give the audience reason to trust an informed and intelligent speaker. Two other elements give the audience reasons to trust a speaker by allowing them to relate to the speaker personally—membership in a community and demonstration of goodwill.

Membership in a community: We tend to trust people who belong to our community because they share our interests, our values, and our concerns. The speaker might show the audience that she belongs to their community by referencing common knowledge. By mentioning information about herself or her past. By confessing interests and values that the community will recognize.

Demonstration of goodwill: We trust people who show us that they have our best interests at heart. The speaker might directly say that he wants to help the audience. Or he might show, through some other gesture, that he wants the audience to prosper. In this textbook, we try to demonstrate goodwill by writing in a friendly manner. A clear and somewhat informal writing style shows that we care about your education. We don't want to flaunt our erudition with abstruse verbiage. (If we did, we'd use more words like "flaunt," "erudition," and "abstruse.") We want to teach so that you can learn.

In sum, we suggest that there are four very common reasons to trust a speaker: (1) She knows the subject. (2) She speaks appropriately to the audience and to the situation. (3) She is part of the audience's community. (4) She bears the audience goodwill. In our discussion, we have focused on elements of writing that can deliver these reasons, but we want to emphasize that other elements in an argument can give the audience a reason to trust the speaker. Music in the background of a car commercial can show the audience that the company knows their taste and belongs to their community—country and western for a commercial that airs in rural Texas, hip-hop for one that plays in Houston. A U.S. flag pin on a senator's lapel shows that she belongs to the national community. Wearing a fleece pullover or a casual shirt (instead of a suit) while touring a disaster site shows that a U.S. president can dress appropriately to the situation. We trust him because he's ready to roll up his sleeves and fix this mess. A reason to trust can be any element that encourages the audience to imagine the speaker as an authority, as a member of the community, as someone who understands the situation, or as someone who cares about the audience.

Further Discussion: On your RHE 306 Canvas site, you'll find persuasive articles about this year's common topic. Choose one to discuss and analyze. Is the author's writing style appropriate to her subject? Does he write about a serious matter in a joking way? Does she show you that she belongs to your community or to the audience's community? Does he seem informed about his subject? How does she show you that she's thoroughly researched this topic? Notice also that many opinion articles published in newspapers include a brief biography of the author. Does the biography (a bit of situated evidence about the speaker) give you additional reason to trust the author?

Reasons to Feel

While reasons to trust focus on the speaker, reasons to feel focus on the subject. A persuasive speaker wants to earn your trust. He also wants to move your emotions. Just as a reason to trust may be dishonest, a reason to feel may be manipulative. Tear-jerker movies prove this to us every day. You come across a manipulative reason to feel anytime you find yourself asking, "Why am I crying at the end of this ridiculous movie?" Nevertheless, just as there are many good reasons to trust a speaker, there are many good reasons to take pride in your country, to love your family, to miss your hometown, and to cherish your friends. To decide what makes a good reason to feel, you must ask yourself, does the object merit the sentiment? Is a romance movie worth crying over? Does a work of art or architecture truly inspire? Does a sex scandal really deserve so much outrage? To find reasons to feel in an argument, you should look for three things: (1) images, (2) values, and (3) honorific or pejorative language.

Images: An image is a visual presentation of something people care about. An image can be a picture or a video. Look at all those sad dogs on the television. They make the audience feel pity. And that pity moves them to attend next week's SPCA-sponsored "adopt-a-pet" event. Look at the pictures of the Washington Monument or the Lincoln Memorial or the Texas Capitol in a textbook for a class on U.S. government. They make the audience feel civic pride. And that pride moves them to vote in next Tuesday's election. Watch the videos of the 9-11 attacks on the World Trade Center. They made a nation so angry we went to war. Sometimes, mere suggestion within a video or film image is extremely moving (a closed casket, a locked door, a distant scream in the night). The audience is left to their vivid imaginations. An image can also be a vivid prose description of something. Instead of showing you the picture, the speaker can explain what it looks like. Sometimes this verbal description is more moving than the picture itself. The speaker can focus and elaborate on details that the audience might overlook.

Values: Images move us by putting things in front of our eyes. *Values* move us by putting things in front of our minds. A value is not tangible. You can't pick it up, look at it, or even touch it. But you care about it nonetheless. Injustice makes you angry. Liberty makes you proud. Ingratitude makes you resentful. None of these things can be touched or photographed. But a speaker can mention them in order to give the audience a reason to feel. If a speaker wants you to feel angry about recent laws that require physicians who perform abortions to have admitting privileges at a hospital, then he might appeal to the value of accessible healthcare:

Further Discussion: Often, vivid description of a real example works two ways. The example is evidence that convinces the audience to believe. The vivid description of the example is a reason to feel. Take the following scenario, and discuss it with your classmates: Imagine you're writing an article that promotes government-subsidized preschool for needy families. You want to show that pre-school deserves to be supported by taxpayer money because it helps kids do well in their first years of school. You could give a statistic: "Studies show that kids who have one year of preschool get on average 65% higher marks on their first- and second-grade benchmark tests for reading and math." That statistic is convincing evidence in support of a reason to believe, but it's not very moving. Think of or find an example that you can vividly describe to move your audience. Try to get your audience to feel happy for one plucky kid who got a leg up. How would you vividly describe that kid's story?

These laws, which claim to protect women's health and well-being, really restrict services. Since so few abortion providers actually have admitting privileges, most will have to close. The remaining clinics will be so few and far between that people living in rural areas will, in effect, be denied medical care. Healthcare, especially reproductive healthcare for women, should be widely available and easily accessible.

Since values cannot be described, they must be explained. A speaker can show that something—such as laws that require hospital admitting privileges for abortion providers—contributes to or takes away from something the audience values—such as accessible healthcare. If certain specific laws detract from accessible healthcare, then the audience will transfer their feelings about accessible healthcare over to these laws. They will feel angry toward anything that threatens accessible healthcare.

To illustrate a value's abstract but moving quality, consider another example: freedom of speech. Speakers have tied the freedom of speech to a range of things that they want us to care about: corporate donations to political action groups; demonstrations at soldiers' funerals; prayer in public schools. Anytime someone insists that an action will allow or hinder freedom of speech, she gives the audience a reason to feel good or bad about that action. A third example illustrates further: a city's unique culture. Anytime someone asks you to "keep Austin weird" by "buying local," he's giving you a reason to like a local store as much as you like the city it's in.

Honorific and Pejorative Language: Here, we encourage you to look at the style of presentation. Speakers use honorific and pejorative language to enhance the emotional impact of an image or a value. *Honorific* language praises something that people already care about (or that they should care about). "Liberty," described honorifically, becomes "our cherished liberty." The Texas Capitol becomes a "magisterial statehouse." *Pejorative* language denounces something that people should already despise. Described pejoratively, conscientious objectors to a war become "draft dodgers." Described pejoratively, regulations on automatic weapons become "threats to our Second-Amendment rights." So far, we have focused on language, but we should emphasize that "honorific" and "pejorative" can apply to many efforts at enhancing the emotions that people already feel. A photographer who wants to honorifically present a public figure will capture him in the best light. A photographer who wants to pejoratively depict the same public figure will zoom in to capture all his wrinkles.

Reasons to Believe

Like reasons to feel, reasons to believe focus on the subject. Rather than asking the audience to experience an emotion, however, reasons to believe ask the audience to arrive at a conclusion. Many theorists of rhetoric will say that a reason to feel is an "emotional appeal," and a reason to believe is a "logical appeal." We don't say "emotion" or "logic" because such terms imply that reasons to feel should be less persuasive than reasons to believe. Calling them "emotional" and "logical" suggests that one type of appeal manipulates the audience. Nothing could be further from the truth. Images and values can both be reasonable, if they deserve to be mentioned and if they apply to the situation. Similarly, a causal or a definitional argument (both appeals to reason) can be foolish. I can say that you should oppose gay marriage because, when we allow homosexuals to legally wed, we open the door to laws that allow people to marry barnyard animals. This, believe it or not, is a "logical" appeal. It asks us to believe that gay marriage will cause humans to marry cows. I can similarly say that you should not feel so attached to traditional marriage because it is a recent invention designed to support the whole wedding-planning industry. Marriage is a scam to sell overpriced diamonds, bad cake, and white dresses. This is a definitional argument, asking you to put traditional marriage in the same category as other tawdry money-making efforts. We suggest that both of these arguments—the causal and the definitional—are unconvincing even though they're reasons to believe. Our point is simple: Reasons to believe can be just as good and just as bad (just as reasonable and just as unreasonable) as reasons to feel.

Reasons to believe can be broken up into different types. In Chapter 8, we explore a few such types of reasons to believe. In this chapter, to help you analyze reasons to believe, we will emphasize the basic form that they all share. Every reason to believe asks the audience to conclude something based on something else. A speaker asks the audience to conclude that another full-blown U.S. war in the Middle East would be an unwinnable mess. She supports this argument by comparing a war in the Middle East to the Vietnam War or to the more recent wars in Afghanistan and Iraq. A speaker asks the audience to conclude that the president of a company should be blamed for its corruption based on the common knowledge that a fish rots from the head down. A speaker asks the audience to conclude that people over the age of 18 should be allowed to drink alcohol because these same people can vote in elections and serve in the military. In each of these cases, you have two elements: a conclusion and a proof. The proof leads to the conclusion. You can paraphrase each reason to believe using a simple template:

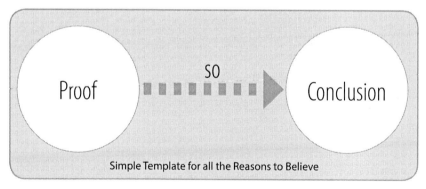

Simple Template for all the Reasons to Believe

Here's how the above reasons to believe translate into the simple template:

- A war in the Middle East would be just like the Vietnam War (or the wars in Afghanistan and Iraq), SO a war in the Middle East would be an unwinnable mess.

- A fish rots from the head down, SO Kenneth Lay was responsible for all the corruption at Enron.
- We let people over the age of 18 vote and serve in the military, SO we should also let them drink alcohol.

While the proof and the conclusion are generally easy to locate, there is often a third hidden element, the *assumption*. This third element is much more difficult to identify because it often remains unstated. Most reasons to believe assume that the audience already believes something else. Based on this assumed belief combined with the proof, the speaker asks the audience to accept the conclusion. Our simple formula, therefore, becomes a bit more complicated:

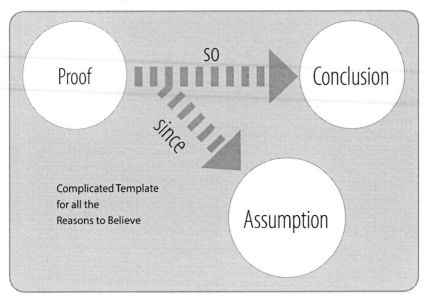

Here's how our reasons translate into this complicated template:

- A war in the Middle East would be just like the Vietnam War in so many ways, SO a war in the Middle East would be an unwinnable mess SINCE all wars that share these qualities must be messy and unwinnable.
- A fish rots from the head down, SO Kenneth Lay was responsible for all the corruption at Enron SINCE as CEO, Lay knew about and directed all of the company's activities.
- We let people over the age of 18 vote and serve in the military SO we should also let them drink alcohol SINCE the privilege to drink alcohol should be given when we confer upon citizens their right to vote and their duty to military service.

Reasons to believe can be the hardest to analyze for two reasons. First, they have the most moving parts. Reasons to trust include efforts to convince the audience that the speaker belongs to a community, is knowledgeable, smart, and good-willed. Reasons to feel include the presentation of images and values (often in pejorative or honorific language). Reasons to believe include three interconnected parts: the proof, the conclusion, and the assumption.

Second, one part of a reason to believe (the assumption) is often not stated, even though it is integral. If the audience does not accept any of the above assumptions, then they will not draw the conclusions based on the proofs. Someone who doesn't believe that all wars sharing certain qualities are just like Vietnam will retort: "Vietnam was a messy war to maintain a puppet government in Southeast Asia; Afghanistan was a difficult effort to establish a new democracy on the Afghan people's terms; and putting troops on the ground in Syria would offer support to people who are fighting against a cruel dictator on the one hand and a violent theocracy on the other. So these are completely different scenarios." Someone who doesn't think that Kenneth Lay knew about Enron's accounting gimmicks will say: "You can't blame Lay for accountants secretly cooking the books. CEOs are figureheads of corporations; they don't really know or direct everything that happens in the organization." And someone who does not think the right to drink should be given along with the right to vote and the duty to serve will say: "Voting and military service are rights and duties of citizenship. They belong together. But drinking is a privilege, like driving a car, and it should not be given to people who won't exercise the privilege responsibly."

Though the assumption may be difficult to locate, it is a very important—maybe the most important—part of any reason to believe. The assumption connects the audience to the argument. If an audience rejects the assumption, then they will reject the conclusion.

Analyzing Reasons

Since the parts of an argument do not announce themselves as reasons, your job is to identify the persuasive elements in a text. We suggest identifying these elements first. Don't worry about labeling them "reasons to trust" or "reasons to feel." Just circle, underline, or describe the parts that you think the audience will notice. Then ask yourself, "Does this paragraph, this image, this sentence, or this video segment try to earn the audience's trust, move their feelings, or guide their beliefs?" Once you've labeled each element a reason to trust, a reason to feel, or a reason to believe, you can explain how one reason relates to the other reasons and to the argument as a whole.

To illustrate, we offer a sample analysis on your RHE 306 Canvas site. We examine the reasons in an argument about the common topic in this year's first-year writing course. To help you further in your efforts at analyzing reasons, below we offer some general advice and pointers.

1. Anything can be a reason. In the first part of this chapter, we tend to focus on bits of printed text, but we also want to note that any persuasive element can be analyzed as a reason to trust, to feel, or to believe: images, music, video clips, color schemes, design templates, and dress styles, and the like.
2. Reasons often work together. As a rhetorical analyst, you must separate the reasons. But you must also show how the reasons work together. For instance, you might explain how the reasons to trust support the reasons to believe. Or how the reasons to feel support the reasons to believe. Or how the reasons to believe support the reasons to trust.
3. One element in an argument can serve as multiple reasons. Several well-researched proofs can lead to one conclusion, thus forming a reason to believe. But these same proofs show the audience that the speaker is knowledgeable, thus forming a reason to trust. An image can move the audience to feel something. But that same image can serve as proof (an example) to support a general conclusion. Thus, one image can simultaneously be a reason to feel and a reason to believe.

Last, we want to explicitly mention the tasks that any rhetorical analyst must do in order to analyze a reason. First, you must locate the persuasive elements in a text. Then, you must identify each element as a kind of reason. Next, you must explain the intended effect on the audience. Finally, you must explain how this reason relates to the others in the argument.

Brief Exercise: The following table breaks down the tasks you should complete whenever you analyze reasons in an argument:

1. Find the persuasive element.	2. Identify this element as a kind of reason.	3. Explain the effect that this reason should have on the audience.	4. Explain how this reason relates to other reasons or to the principal claim.
Johnson describes recent terrorist activities.	Reason to feel	It convinces the audience to feel fear.	The fear that the audience feels about terrorism leads them to feel fearful about potential terrorists buying guns.
Johnson explains that people who are currently under suspicion for terrorist-related activities can still purchase firearms without restriction.	Reason to believe	It convinces the audience to believe that potential terrorists have access to powerful weapons.	The belief that terrorists can buy weapons without restriction and the fear of terrorism both combine to support Johnson's argument that people on the government's "no-fly" list for terrorist suspects should also be restricted from purchasing firearms.

Make a similar table about the text you've decided to analyze. You will probably find more reasons than you could possibly analyze in a 4–5 page paper. So think about which reasons are most important or most interesting, and focus on those in your analysis.

CHAPTER 6

Evidence That People Find

I n the last chapter, we discussed the reasons that a speaker can invent to support a claim. We mentioned that evidence often supports such reasons. For example, if you are trying to persuade your friend to prepare for an exam by studying a little bit every night rather than cramming, you might invent a few reasons:

1. Studying for exams a little bit at a time results in better grades, so you should study for thirty minutes every night this week.
2. I'm a good student. You should trust my advice.
3. You'll enjoy your half-hour study sessions. They're relaxed. Nothing is more pleasant than reading over your notes and practicing a few calculus problems while enjoying a chai latte at the coffee shop down the road. You could do that every morning!

In our imagined example, there is a reason to believe that certain study habits result in good grades, a reason to trust the speaker, and a reason to feel good about studying every day. The reason to believe seems a bit weak, however. Your friend may wonder, "How do you know that studying every day will lead to better grades? Do you know Eddie? That guy crams for every exam. And he's a straight-A student!" Your friend has evidence—an example—to support her argument. As a result, she favors cramming. You can counter with evidence of your own: examples of people who study every day and proof that Eddie studies every day, despite what he says. All of your additional evidence supports that first reason to believe: Studying for exams a little bit at a time results in better grades, so you should study for thirty minutes every night this week

Often, evidence supports reasons, which themselves support a claim. Evidence, however, may directly support a claim. Returning to our example, imagine that you add to your argument the following evidence: Professor Glimson says the best way to learn calculus is by practicing a little bit every day. This evidence directly supports your claim that daily study is preferable to cramming. The diagram below illustrates how some of your evidence supports a reason and some of your evidence supports the claim.

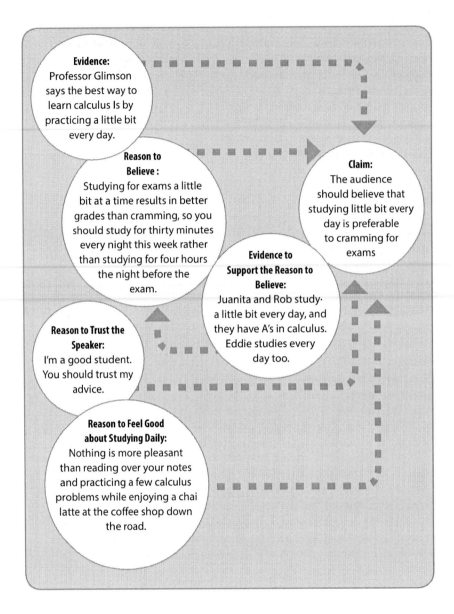

We open with this example to explain the difference between reasons and evidence and to show you the basic steps that you should follow when analyzing evidence.

- **First, separate the reasons from the evidence.** The descriptions of reasons and evidence in this chapter and in the last chapter will help you to separate one from the other.
- **Second, explain what the evidence is doing.** Is it there to make a reason more convincing, or is it there to directly support the argument? Keep in mind that one

piece of evidence can accomplish many things. The example of Juanita studying every day supports the reason to believe that daily study is effective. But that example also vividly describes an image of Juanita at Prufrock's coffee shop smiling as she leisurely sips on a macchiato and finishes last night's calculus homework. Juanita's image supports the reason to feel good about studying daily. The example accomplishes two rhetorical purposes, making the audience believe and encouraging the audience to feel.

- **Third, explain why the evidence is needed.** If an audience already accepts something as true, then further evidence isn't needed to convince them. If an audience doubts that something is true, then evidence is necessary. But evidence doesn't strictly address a dubious audience. It may help the audience to imagine something they cannot yet conceptualize. It may help them feel something more strongly. For instance, an audience may already dislike gun-related violence. But in order to gain their support for an assault-weapons ban, the speaker needs to make them feel horrified, so he offers statistics about the number of people killed with automatic or semi-automatic rifles in the last three years. The argument doesn't need to convince a doubtful audience. They already agree that many people die in gun-related violence, and they agree that it's a problem. But they don't feel strongly enough about these particular weapons. So the argument includes statistical evidence to incite the audience's outrage.

While exploring these basic steps, this introductory gambit also demonstrates why the speaker's specific research and broad knowledge are so important. Often, we imagine persuasive people as slick media blowhards who don't know what they're talking about or silver-tongued used-car salesmen who can't tell the difference between a radiator and a carburetor. Without a doubt, such people exist, and they can be persuasive despite their ignorance. However, more often than not, the persuasive speaker has done her research. Furthermore, she has acquired a broad education about a range of subjects. Careful research provides her with evidence. Broad knowledge helps her to connect with the audience. Below, we offer categories that identify certain kinds of evidence. But we caution against believing that, once a speaker knows the kinds of evidence, she can be persuasive. To be persuasive, a speaker needs to know the evidence itself. She must also know how to present the evidence in a convincing argument.

Types of Evidence

Like reasons, evidence comes in all shapes and sizes. To make things even more complicated, we keep inventing new kinds of evidence. When you choose a major, you decide to study the ways of collecting evidence in biology, chemistry, history, or psychology. Since we cannot cover all or even most of the kinds of evidence, we will instead focus on a few of the more common types of evidence that you are likely to find in public arguments. These categories will help you to analyze the texts you've selected for your second major assignment.

Authority: In Chapter 2, we briefly discuss authority. Authorities are the experts whom you can cite when you lack expertise. Let's imagine you're not a family psychologist, but you want to prove that adoption laws should favor traditionally married couples because they tend to raise well-adjusted children. You can quote a respected family psychologist.

Authorities are very useful, especially if the audience recognizes and trusts the expertise of the authorities. But if the audience doesn't know about such things, then the authorities must be introduced to show why they deserve the audience's trust. A speaker may introduce an authority by saying, for instance, "According to respected family psychologist Pilar Hernandez, traditionally married couples who adopt are more likely to raise emotionally adjusted children." If the audience still won't trust Hernandez's authority, then additional introductory information may be needed: "According to Pilar Hernandez, a respected family psychologist who has written several books on the subject of children's emotional development in adoptive families, couples in a traditional marriage are more likely to raise well-adjusted children." To counter such an argument, you should find authorities who say the opposite: psychiatrists who find that an adopted child's emotional development has no connection to the parents' gender or sexuality.

An authority can speak outside of his expertise and still be trusted. U.S. presidents and governors often stand as authorities on morality, even though they are experts on government. Religious leaders stand as authorities on politics, even though they are experts on theology. And athletes stand as authorities on everything from parenting to world affairs, even though they are experts on professional sports. Not long ago, a former vice president with training as a lawyer gave world-renowned lectures on global climate change. And a real-estate magnate became a major contender for national political office. Al Gore was no expert on the subject of climatology, but people trusted what he had to say. Donald Trump is no authority on international affairs, yet people have supported his campaign for the U.S. presidency.

Of course, an audience should trust an authority based on his or her expertise, but this doesn't mean that people trust an authority only in the area of his or her expertise. People often conclude that a person's excellence in one aspect of life will translate elsewhere. It is for this reason that we often elect military and civic leaders to political office. And we ask religious leaders for advice about raising a family. When rhetorically analyzing a speaker's use of authority as evidence, you should worry less about whether the authority is really an expert on a given subject and instead focus on whether and why an audience would trust this authority. If the audience will not initially trust this person, then what can the speaker say to show that the authority deserves the audience's trust?

Testimony: Testimony and authority are similar. Both rely on something someone else said. The following two examples capture the difference between authority and testimony:

1. A medical doctor who works in a drug-treatment facility says that abusing prescription medication often leads to the abuse of illegal narcotics. She is an *authority*, someone who has expert knowledge.
2. An addict says that he started using OxyContin to treat a neck injury, but he graduated to heroin when he discovered that it satisfied his craving more effectively and more cheaply. The addict is no expert. He hasn't studied narcotics, nor has he worked for years treating addicts. But he has personal experience. The addict offers *testimony*, a personal account of something he lived or witnessed firsthand.

Testimony can be more convincing than authority. Experts can sound detached. They have a lot of information, but they may not have experienced anything directly, so their knowledge can seem sterile. We trust people who have seen and survived. When you want advice about how to get over a break-up, you'll ask your older sister before you ask a trained psychologist. Your sister, as you know, has experienced heartache. The psychologist read a textbook about emotional distress due to infidelity. When you want advice about how to write a poem, you will ask a poet, not a literary critic. The poet has wrestled with words. He knows firsthand what it's like to struggle with a line or a stanza. The literary critic knows about some poets who struggled with lines or stanzas.

Both testimony and authority can support reasons to believe. These two forms of evidence can also offer reasons to trust a speaker. Audiences trust authorities because of their expertise. A speaker who can cite such an authority borrows the authority's expertise and earns the audience's trust. Audiences trust testimony because it comes from people with firsthand experience. By citing the person who saw things firsthand, a speaker can borrow that experience and earn the audience's trust. Even if you don't know or haven't seen, the audience can trust you because you've at least spoken to people who know and have seen.

Testimony is particularly well suited to move the audience's emotions. We will not be moved to tears of joy when a psychologist tells us that wedding ceremonies elicit gleeful sentiment in 98% of the parents who attend. But we may choke up as we listen to the father of the groom describe what he felt while watching his son say his marriage vows. Because testimony has such emotional impact, many newspaper stories open with something journalists call a "human interest lead" before offering statistical information. A journalist may write a paragraph or two describing and quoting a disaster victim or homeless person. Then, he might present statistics about the number of people who lost their homes to a tornado or the number of people sleeping on the streets tonight.

Example: Examples are particular people, things, moments, or places that the speaker brings forward. Examples can serve many rhetorical purposes. An image of a few starving children in a faraway country can move the audience to feel pity. A description of a man's journey across the Pacific Ocean on a raft can move the audience to believe that ancient peoples could have migrated by sea from the Pacific islands to California. A summary of a book that someone has written can earn the audience's trust that the speaker is an authority. Each of the previous sentences offers a *hypothetical* example—something specific that didn't actually exist—and each of these hypothetical examples aims to convince you to believe the broader claim at the beginning of this paragraph: "Examples serve many purposes." Our point is that examples don't have to be vivid. They don't have to be typical. And they don't have to be real. An example only has to be specific: one person, one event, one place, one thing.

Different kinds of examples typically serve different rhetorical purposes. Here are some of the more common rhetorical uses of examples:

- *Vivid examples* typically aim to move the audience's emotions by offering an image.
- *Hypothetical (not real) examples* typically aim to show the audience something that they have not yet imagined.
- *Real examples*, especially when offered in abundance, typically aim to convince the audience to believe that something is possible or even typical.

Because it is so versatile, the example is one of the most common forms of evidence. Even statistical data are an elaborate collection of examples to prove that a trend exists. How do you know that women favor one political candidate over another? The statistician offers a survey—examples of 1,000 women, randomly surveyed: 57.2% (572 specific women) saying they would vote for Emily Chao.

Since examples are so common and so versatile, it is important not only to identify an example but also to explain its rhetorical purpose. Does the example support the principal claim or one of the reasons? And how does the example offer that support?

Sign: A sign is an indication that something may exist or be true. Clouds in the sky are signs that it will rain. Wet pavement is a sign that rain has recently fallen. Neither clouds nor the wet street is an example of rain. But they can indicate rain. Sometimes signs are quite trustworthy. Sometimes not. A sign of pregnancy is weight gain. But it's not a very trustworthy sign, since people's bodies change for all sorts of reasons. A better sign of pregnancy is lactation. But that's not foolproof either. To determine whether a sign will be persuasive, you should think about the audience. Will they accept something as a reliable indication of something else? A scientist must wonder *whether the indication is reliable*. A speaker—and a rhetorical analyst—must wonder *whether the audience will believe that it's reliable*.

Signs, like examples, can serve many rhetorical purposes. Here are two of the more common rhetorical uses of signs:

- *Indications of fact*: Signs often encourage the audience to believe that certain things exist or have existed. How do we know the economy is doing better? Look at the stock market's recent performance. How do we know the economy is not improving for most people? Look at the levels of unemployment. How do we know the economy has not done well for the last few years? Look at the slow growth in gross domestic product.

- *Harbingers of the future:* Signs often ask the audience to feel something—often hope or fear. Omens, for example, are bad signs. Many believe that a dip in the consumer confidence index is an omen of another economic downturn. Others believe that a high trade deficit is an omen of a country's impending economic decline.

As the above examples illustrate, signs are far from certain. But their uncertainty should not lead us or anyone else to doubt them altogether. Much contemporary science relies on signs. The chief evidence for the existence of other planets is the example of our own solar system (which must be typical) and two signs: a visible wobble and an occasional shadow that we can detect when observing distant stars. The chief evidence for global climate change is a range of signs: increased rainfall in some regions, slight upticks in overall temperature, diminishing ice at the polar caps.

Maxim: The previous two types of evidence—examples and signs—call upon what we can see in the world around us. Testimony and authority depend on experts in a community. Maxims and fables, on the other hand, depend upon wisdom in a society. A maxim is a phrase that captures something believed by almost everyone:

- A stitch in time saves nine. (If you do something at the appropriate moment, then you won't have to work harder later on to fix the problems caused by poor timing.)
- Many eyes make all bugs shallow. (When more people are looking at a project, its problems become much more evident.)
- Revenge is a dish best served cold. (If you want to get back at someone, you should wait until you can calmly plan your revenge.)
- An ounce of prevention is worth a pound of cure. (A little effort to prevent a problem is the same as a lot of effort to fix the problem.)
- It has jumped the shark. (When a story has to resort to ridiculous plot gimmicks to keep the audience interested, its time has passed.)

As the above maxims demonstrate, each specific expression requires cultural knowledge. You won't know what "An ounce of prevention is worth a pound of cure" means unless someone at some time explained it to you. You're more likely to know the expression if you work in the medical industry, where people regularly repeat it. You won't know what "It has jumped the shark" means unless you're familiar with the last seasons of the 1970s sitcom *Happy Days*, and even then some explanation may be needed. And unless you're familiar with the open-source movement in software engineering, you won't understand what is meant by "Many eyes make all bugs shallow." Because maxims require so much cultural knowledge, older and more experienced people tend to have larger collections of these phrases. Since wise people know maxims, a speaker's ability to use a maxim appropriately will give the audience a reason to trust her as a wise authority.

Brief Exercise: Rhetoric students once collected maxims in what were called "commonplace books." They gathered cultural wisdom that they could use when making arguments. For a week, keep a notebook and a pen at hand. When you hear an expression that you've heard before and that carries resonance with you or someone else, write it down. Then paraphrase the meaning. You'll be surprised at how much commonplace wisdom hides in the little expressions that people use every day.

To an audience who knows and believes a maxim, the expression can be very convincing. Rather than researching examples of excellent students who study early, I can say: "Instead of cramming for eight hours, you should study thirty minutes a day this week. After all, a stitch in time saves nine."

Fable: A fable, like a maxim, captures a bit of cultural wisdom. Maxims package such wisdom in sentences. Fables package it in stories. Consider the well-known fable of the tortoise and the rabbit. The tortoise is slow. The rabbit is fast. The rabbit makes fun of the tortoise and challenges him to a race. The tortoise accepts. During the race, the rabbit runs far ahead and decides that he can take a nap. The tortoise steadily crawls to the finish line and wins the race. What wisdom is captured in this story? There's the typical maxim: "Slow and steady wins the race." There's also another moral: Don't believe you're so good that you don't have to try.

Many fables about mythical talking creatures are attributed to Aesop, of ancient Greece, but some fables come to us as fairy tales, such as those recorded by the brothers Wilhelm and Jacob Grimm (a.k.a. Grimm's fairy tales). Their story about Hansel and Gretel reminds children not to wander too far or eat too much candy. Some fables are apocryphal stories told about history. George Washington did not chop down a cherry tree when he was a boy, nor did he say to his father, "I cannot tell a lie." Nevertheless, we tell this fable to remind ourselves that great leaders should be honest. The Dutch who settled Manhattan did not buy the island for a handful of beads. (The Canarsee tribe accepted many gifts in exchange for the land's temporary use.) But we tell the story to remind ourselves that a profitable real estate transaction often involves a shrewd buyer and an ignorant seller. Finally, fables aren't restricted to arguments about morality. Astronomers echo a well-known fable every time they call the distance between the Earth and the Sun the "Goldilocks zone." The moral: The middle—not too hot, not too cold—is the best.

How can a fable serve as evidence? If the audience knows a story and accepts its basic lesson, then the speaker can apply the story's lesson to a new situation. Even if the audience doesn't know a fable, however, the story can be very persuasive. Fables get repeated because they are full of drama, intrigue, memorable characters, and delicious plot twists. To convince you that you should study every day instead of cramming,

I could tell the story of the three little pigs, which you likely know. I could say that cramming the night before is like building a house out of straw or sticks—trying to make a solid foundation out of minimal effort and shoddy materials. The person who studies every day, on the other hand, builds a house out of brick.

Or I could tell you Aesop's fable of the ant and the grasshopper:

> Every day in the spring, the ant collects a little bit of food and stores it away. The grasshopper sings and dances, eating only what he needs and saving nothing. When winter comes, the ant survives while the grasshopper starves. The moral: To work today is to eat tomorrow. The same lesson applies to studying: To learn everyday is to know tomorrow.

Even if you've never heard the fable of the ant and the grasshopper before, you might be convinced by the story because the characters are typical—the creature who plays foolishly and the creature who works diligently. And the results are predictable—playing leads to poverty, and working leads to prosperity. Mentioning that Aesop first told the story centuries ago adds to its persuasive ability. After all, even though he wrote about insects, Aesop was an authority on human morality.

Analyzing Evidence

On your RHE 306 Canvas site, we offer a sample analysis that focuses on an argument that is relevant to this year's common topic. We suggest that you read this example to see how analyzing evidence can support an argument.

In what remains of this chapter, we want to offer a basic process for analyzing evidence: First, identify the pieces of evidence; second, relate those pieces of evidence to the reasons or to the principal claim in the argument; third, label the evidence using the terms in this chapter; fourth, analyze the relationships among the evidence, the argument, and the audience. An easy four steps to a good analysis! Perhaps not. It is not always necessary to follow the order that we suggest or to complete all the steps that we outline. And sometimes you may have to go back and repeat one or two of the steps. But the process should at least highlight the things that a careful analysis will accomplish. A careful analysis will show where the evidence is. It will explain how the evidence contributes to the reasons and the claim. It will explain what kind of evidence is in the argument. And it will explain how the evidence relates to the audience.

Further Discussion: People retell fables to teach new lessons. Think about the story of Rapunzel. For many years, this story taught young girls that they should be obedient to their parents and that they should wait for a prince to rescue them from bad circumstances. The movie *Tangled* retells the fable. What's the new lesson? Can you think of another fable that has been retold to teach a new bit of cultural wisdom?

We also want to point out that, even though we suggest analyzing the reasons first, the evidence may take up the largest part of the argument. Some arguments overflow with evidence, much of it in support of a single reason. As mentioned much earlier in this chapter, if someone wanted to prove that global climate change is really happening, he could point to a litany of signs: rising sea levels, changing weather patterns, increased temperatures, decreased ice at the North and South Poles. Listing all this evidence would take pages, but it would all serve the same reason to believe: Many signs indicate a permanent shift in the world's climate, so you should believe that global climate change is really happening. Take another hypothetical example. Imagine someone wants to prove that the U.S. electorate is becoming more conservative. She could point to many examples—surveys and interviews with voters—to show that many people hold conservative beliefs. She could point to recent elections won by Republicans— signs that the voters favor conservative candidates. And she could cite political pundits—authorities—who all say that the "silent majority" in America is conservative. This evidence could fill an entire book, even though it would all support the one claim.

Finally, we want to emphasize that evidence, like reasons, is audience-specific. It is easy to imagine evidence—especially certain kinds of evidence—as universally persuasive. Who would doubt statistics from the U.S. census, images from the Hubble telescope, or data from the Large Hadron Collider? Though such evidence may be unassailable, it is not universally convincing, nor is it always necessary. You can tell an audience that there are as many stars in the sky as there are grains of sand on the beach without showing elaborate images of the universe. They will likely believe you without the evidence. And you can tell people that the Large Hadron Collider created a quark-gluon plasma that scientists could use to test for supersymmetry, and the audience will not understand you. (We don't even understand what that means.) Our point is that different kinds and amounts of evidence are needed for different audiences, depending on what each audience believes, feels, understands, and has experienced. When analyzing evidence, your job is to show the connection to the audience. And the same is true of all rhetorical analysis. Rhetorical analysis explains how a text relates to specific people in a given place at a particular time.

Brief Exercise: Play Evidence Bingo! In small groups, using the cards below (or cards you make up yourselves), read several articles out loud. Everytime someone spots a kind of evidence, shout out its name. If you have a square on your card that lists the name of that kind of evidence, put an X on the square. The first person to have three in a row wins!

Card for Player 1

Hypothetical example	Expert Authority	Sign (omen)
Testimony	Maxim	Vivid Example
Statistics	Sign (indication of fact)	Fable

Card for Player 2

Expert Authority	Vivid Example	Testimony
Maxim	Real Example	Sign (omen)
Statistics	Fable	Hypothetical Example

Card for Player 3

Statistics	Testimony	Sign (omen)
Fable	Expert Authority	Sign (indication of fact)
Maxim	Hypothetical Example	Vivid Example

Card for Player 4

Real Example	Testimony	Vivid Example
Fable	Maxim	Sign (indication of fact)
Sign (omen)	Hypothetical Example	Statistics

Card for Player 5

Real Example	Maxim	Statistics
Sign (indication of fact)	Vivid Example	Testimony
Sign (omen)	Fable	Hypothetical Example

CHAPTER 7 | Analyzing the Argument and the Audience

N o rhetorical analysis can explain the relationships among every element in the text and every part of the context. So you should focus on a few interesting textual features and a few salient parts of the situation. For instance, your rhetorical analysis might try to explain how the reasons address recent events, how the evidence appeals to the audience, how the speaker uses what the audience already knows to convince them of a claim they don't yet believe, or how images move the audience's emotions.

In Chapters 4–6, we offered tools for labeling the elements of the context—speaker, audience, and situation—and for labeling the elements of the argument—claim, reasons, and evidence. In this chapter, we offer strategies for relating these elements to one another. Specifically, we offer strategies for analyzing the relationship between the argument and the audience. A good rhetorical analysis paper must accomplish all of these tasks. It must label the important elements in the text; it must point out the relevant parts of the context; and it must explain how these textual and contextual parts fit together into a persuasive (or an unpersuasive) argument.

Relating the Reasons and the Evidence to the Audience

Every reason and every bit of evidence must be presented to an audience, and the audience will decide whether the reason or the evidence is persuasive. If an audience agrees to all the reasons and all the evidence, then they will be completely persuaded. But complete assent is not necessary. In fact, complete assent is quite rare. Think of how many times you find yourself saying, "Well, I don't agree with everything that person says, but enough of it makes sense to me, so I'll agree to do what she recommends."

An argument can convince an audience even though some of the reasons or some of the evidence doesn't move them at all. Imagine that you are trying to convince a friend that the state of Texas should continue to offer in-state tuition to people who can't prove their legal residency in the U.S. You invent the following reasons:

- People who live, work, and pay taxes in Texas deserve the same benefits, regardless of their citizenship status, so we should ask everyone who lives in Texas to pay the same in-state tuition.

- It would be unfair to tell someone who grew up in Texas that she must pay more for college tuition just because her parents brought her into this country illegally when she was six months old.
- Giving in-state tuition to everyone that resides in the state will ensure that more of the talented people raised in Texas remain in Texas. No matter where they come from, talented people who get college degrees will earn more money, pay more in taxes, and ultimately benefit everyone.
  - There is evidence to support this reason. Dr. Reynaldo García estimates that Texas tax revenue would increase 23% if undocumented immigrants could earn college degrees and work in the state. And he further estimates that the economy would grow annually by an additional 2.4%.
- Think about how much you value college and how much you hope to benefit from your education. Would you take that opportunity away from someone just because of his citizenship status?

You have four reasons and one bit of evidence (authority). After you make your arguments, your friend says that there is nothing "fair" or "right" about giving the benefits of citizenship to "illegals." She's not sympathetic to lawbreakers. So she's not moved by your first, second, or your last reasons. You realize that the first, second, and last reasons will appeal to an audience with certain qualities: an audience that thinks all state residents, regardless of citizenship, deserve the same treatment; an audience that thinks it's fair to treat everyone who works hard equally; an audience that feels sympathy for all people who aspire to improve their lives.

Your audience—your friend—does not feel such sympathy, nor does she assume such things. But she confesses that your third reason is persuasive. She says, "I don't want people to benefit because of something they've done illegally, but I see that the state could prosper if we let illegal aliens get an education and contribute to the economy." She's not convinced, but she's moved. Perhaps, you could offer further evidence or counterarguments to support your first, second, and/or last reasons. Even if she never feels sympathy, she might accept that paying in-state tuition (like having a driver's license) has nothing to do with U.S. citizenship, so it's not a "right" but rather a "privilege." If she accepts your first and your third reasons, then she might reluctantly accept the entire argument, even if she never feels the sympathy that you tried to evoke.

Our point is that an argument doesn't need to completely convince an audience of everything that the speaker says. Assent is a matter of degree. When rhetorically analyzing an argument, you can measure how much assent the argument will generate by determining how much of the evidence and how many of the reasons the audience will accept. For each piece of evidence, you must ask: Will this audience accept this example? Will they know this maxim? Will they enjoy and believe this fable's moral? For each reason, you must wonder: Will the audience be moved to feel something, or will they trust or believe the speaker based on what the speaker says? And you must explain why the audience would or would not accept each reason or each piece of evidence.

When explaining why you think the audience will or will not accept an argument's reasons and evidence, you may rely on the *textual information* that you find in the argument itself. You may decide, for instance, that because your third reason is supported by copious evidence, it is more likely to convince. The amount of evidence supporting that third reason is textual because you find it in the text itself. But you should also consider finding some *contextual information* to support your claims. A bit of research might reveal that your friend has demonstrated a lack of sympathy for anyone who came into this country illegally. Maybe she wrote a letter to the editor of your college newspaper saying as much. This kind of contextual information demonstrates something about the audience, and this information helps you to more convincingly explain her reactions. The letter to the editor might prove that she is not at all tolerant of people she calls "criminals." And her disposition explains her reluctance to entertain some of your reasons.

Relating the Reasons and the Evidence to One Another

As we've explained so far, one strategy for rhetorical analysis is to explain how each piece of evidence and each reason will convince—or fail to convince—the audience. This strategy can explain why the audience may agree with the principal claim even though they do not appreciate all the evidence or every reason. Furthermore, this

Brief Exercise: Make a list of all the reasons and evidence you find in the text you've chosen to analyze. Then, next to each item in your list, explain how you think the audience will react to this discrete part of the argument. Next to your prediction of the audience's reaction, explain why you think they are likely to have this reaction. Finally, next to each explanation, give textual and/or contextual information to support your claim. You can format your list as a table like this one:

Reason	Audience's Reaction	Explanation of Audience's Reaction	Textual Information	Contextual Information
Reason to feel sympathy for undocumented immigrants who aspire to improve their lives: "Think about how much you value college and how much you hope to benefit from your education. Would you take that opportunity away from someone just because of his citizenship status?"	Not persuaded	Kaitlyn does not feel sympathetic toward anyone who has come into this country illegally.	There is no evidence to support this reason.	In a letter to the editor of the *Daily Texan*, Kaitlyn said, "Anyone who crosses the U.S. border illegally is a criminal, so we shouldn't feel bad when they aren't treated like U.S. citizens."

strategy can explain how much an audience is likely to be persuaded. Such an analysis assumes, however, that the audience will see all the evidence and all the reasons at the same time, which is rarely the case. Typically, an audience will notice one thing, then something else, and then something else. Even visual arguments happen in a sequence. Every video has a beginning, a middle, and an end. Paintings and billboards initially draw your attention to particular elements. Most viewers will look at the various parts of an image in a common order. Most importantly, an argument's sequential presentation changes the audience, preparing them psychologically for what comes next.

To illustrate, here's a hypothetical example: While driving down the highway, you see a billboard with a gruesome image of two cars in a head-on collision. You're horrified. This emotion prompts you to read the words adjacent to the picture: "Talk, Text, Crash!" The strong feelings induced by the image have led you to read the words as a warning. If you read the words before seeing the image, they will not have their intended (emotionally persuasive) effect. The sequence of reasons is important. First, you must encounter the reason to feel horror (the image of the two cars crumpled against one another). Then you must read the words to believe that you shouldn't use your phone while driving. These three words are an abbreviated reason to believe that talking on the phone or texting while driving will distract you and cause you to get in a wreck. If you simply encounter the reason to believe, you'll be more likely to dismiss it by saying, "That never really happens," or "That won't happen to me because I'm careful." But once you have the vivid image of a horrible crash in mind, it's much more difficult to dismiss the warning.

Instead of trying to understand how the audience will respond to each discrete element, your rhetorical analysis—like our very brief analysis of a hypothetical billboard—can explain how the reasons and the evidence fit together, that is, how each element (each reason or piece of evidence) prepares the audience for the next. How does the audience react to one piece of evidence or one reason, and why will that reaction make them more or less likely to accept the next piece of evidence or the next reason?

Sequential analysis (looking at how each reason or each piece of evidence sets up the next) can explain some things overlooked by *holistic analysis* (looking at all the reasons and all the evidence at once). Holistic analysis cannot explain why an audience that is predisposed to reject a particular reason might be brought around to accepting it. For further illustration, let's return to your friend Kaitlyn, who does not want the state of Texas to charge illegal immigrants in-state tuition. If you open your argument by asking her to sympathize with undocumented immigrants, then you will likely get nowhere. But if you begin with a reason that she is more likely to accept, then you might slowly cajole her into sympathizing with people she has elsewhere called "criminal." You know that she wants the Texas economy to improve, so you begin by saying that helping undocumented immigrants to attend college will boost economic growth. Then you mention that these same would-be college students likely will live in Texas after they graduate and will contribute to the state's vibrant business culture. You offer an example of a student who plans to attend UT and major in agricultural science so that she can improve methods of irrigation and help Texas farmers to survive drought years. Once you've vividly described this example of one person, you give your friend a reason to sympathize: "Doesn't Analise deserve an opportunity to excel and to give back to the community?" Your opening reason sets up an example, which then leads into an emotional appeal for sympathy.

Sequential analysis relates the reasons and the evidence to one another by showing how each reason or each bit of evidence draws on previous elements and contributes to later elements. Like holistic analysis, sequential analysis requires that you first identify the speaker, the audience, the situation, the reasons, and the evidence. But the two strategies differ in one key regard. Holistic analysis assumes that the audience doesn't change as they receive the argument. Sequential analysis assumes that the audience must change as they receive the argument. Both assumptions are valid. No argument will completely change anyone's mind, but every argument can change its audience a little bit. You have to decide what you want to emphasize in your rhetorical analysis. The analytic strategy that you choose—holistic or sequential—should reflect your decision.

Brief Exercise: Make a flowchart of the argument that you want to analyze. Use arrows to represent evidence and reasons. Place a box after each arrow to show what the audience should think or feel at that particular moment in the argument's progression. Use a triangle below each box to explain how the audience's reaction prepares them for the next bit of evidence or the next reason. Follow the example presented below:

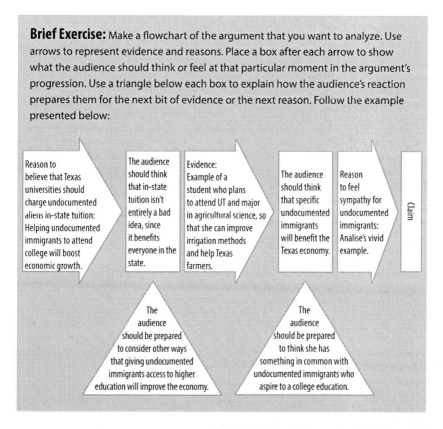

General Advice about Writing a Rhetorical Analysis

Though there are many ways to analyze the rhetoric in any text, every rhetorical analysis must accomplish four tasks:

- **Summarize or describe the text**. Keep in mind that you're writing to an audience who may not have seen the image, watched the video, or read the article that you're analyzing. Even if your readers have seen the text, they may have forgotten or overlooked the elements (the reasons and the evidence) that you think are most important. So you will have to remind them. You do not have to summarize or describe every detail, but you should give your reader a general sense of the principal claim, the main reasons, and the key evidence in the argument.
- **Describe the audience, situation, and speaker**. Since you're ultimately trying to explain how the text relates to the context, you should describe the context and its most important features. Even if your reader knows who the speaker is, some reminding will be helpful.
- **Label the salient elements of the text**. Labeling reasons and evidence will highlight the most persuasive parts of the text. More importantly, such labeling will show how these parts work in the argument. Do not feel obligated to label every piece of evidence or every reason. Focus on the reasons and the evidence that you think are most important or that you find most interesting.
- **Analyze the relationships between the text and the context**. As we mention at the beginning of this chapter, rhetorical analysis ultimately aims at this last task. Nevertheless, you probably will not spend the majority of your time analyzing. You might dedicate many words to summarizing and labeling. Summarizing and labeling are the heavy lifting that set up those crucial sentences where you explain how these textual and contextual elements fit together.

Brief Exercise: On your RHE 306 Canvas site is a sample student Rhetorical Analysis paper. Find highlighters or pens of four different colors. Assign each color to a particular task in rhetorical analysis. For instance: red—summarizing or describing the text; blue—describing the audience, situation, and speaker; yellow—labeling the salient textual elements; orange—analyzing the relationship between the text and the context. Read the sample student paper, paying attention to each sentence and its purpose. Ask yourself, "Does this sentence summarize the text, describe the audience, label the textual elements, or analyze the relationship between text and context?" Highlight each sentence using the color that corresponds to the task the sentence attempts to fulfill. When you finish reading the paper, notice how much space the student dedicates to each task. Did she dedicate significantly more words to any one particular task? Should she have dedicated fewer or more words to any of the tasks?

CHAPTER 8 | Inventing Arguments

You probably learned to solve algebraic equations in high school or college. Perhaps you learned to construct valid syllogisms from a logic textbook. You certainly learned to do long division from your elementary- and middle-school math teachers. But where did you learn to argue? In high school and middle school, you may have taken a course that taught you the basics: making a claim, presenting evidence, and inventing reasons. But that brief exposure can't account for your skill. And the truth is, even before middle school, you were probably very good at arguing. That's because everyone learns to argue from a very young age, not in formal classes, not from textbooks, and not from teachers. Most of us were still in diapers when we learned to say "No!" From that moment on, we practiced argumentation.

Of course, some forms of argumentation require formal instruction: syllogistic logic, symbolic logic, any form of mathematics. And every discipline—every major in college— teaches a kind of argumentation. Nonetheless, even as we formally learn specific kinds of argumentation, we continue to share an informal manner of arguing. If everyone already knows and is proficient in informal argumentation, then there is no need for us to teach you anything. Whenever you want to prove a point, you start to look for reasons, and you find them easily. Since we can't promise to teach you anything that you don't already know, we'll promise to sharpen the argumentative tools you already have.

Let's imagine that you want to invent some reasons to support your claim that criminal background checks should be required for every gun buyer in the United States. You think about it for a while. Here's what you come up with:

- Criminal background checks will not interrupt any law-abiding citizen's ability to acquire firearms.
- Criminal background checks will reduce the amount of gun-related violence in the United States by keeping guns out of the hands of criminals.
- If people have to undergo criminal background checks to qualify for jobs in law enforcement and transportation security, then shouldn't they similarly have to pass these checks before buying a gun?

These are common arguments that you've heard elsewhere. There are, of course, other ways to think about the matter. And you learn these other arguments when you hear someone arguing against criminal background checks for gun buyers with the following reasons:

- Criminal background checks will be impossible at gun shows. Many estimate that 40% of all U.S. gun sales happen at gun shows. So requiring criminal background checks will interrupt many people's ability purchase firearms.
- Criminal background checks will not keep guns out of the hands of criminals. Criminals will rely on straw-purchases (getting someone to buy a gun for them), as they already do. States with strict laws that restrict gun sales (such as California) do not have notably lower rates of gun-related violence.
- A criminal background check for transportation security and law-enforcement is perfectly reasonable. People who keep us safe and enforce the law should have no criminal past. But guns are largely purchased for self-protection and sport. Hunters and people who want to feel safe in their homes should not have to undergo a criminal background check, anymore than someone who wants to buy a compound bow or pepper spray.

How can you resolve this debate? You could search for more evidence. There are certainly examples of and statistics about the correlation between strict gun laws and gun-related crime. But these examples and statistics are not conclusive. People with no criminal history, people who legally acquired their guns, occasionally go on shooting sprees. Delaware has fairly restrictive gun-control laws, yet Delaware residents die in gun-related violence about as often (per capita) as the residents of Texas where the gun-control laws are comparatively permissive. More importantly, no examples or statistics can tell us once and for all how to define an "imposition on someone's Second Amendment rights." And no expert authority can say for certain what will happen if we require criminal background checks for all gun purchases in the US. If only you could respond to your opponent without resorting to evidence. If only you could think of more reasons.

You're in luck! Rhetoric teachers in antiquity and today have taught students to invent reasons by reviewing the topics of argumentation. Ancient rhetoric teachers thought of the topics as places someone can visit to find reasons. For this reason, in this chapter, when we talk about you using a topic to invent an argument, we say you "invent an argument *at the topic of...*" We talk about it as if you were physically in the place where the argument can be found. In this chapter, we explore six topics of argumentation to help you invent reasons that will support any claim. A student who knows these topics and can invent arguments using these and other topics will never run out of things to say. She will be able to argue more carefully and more effectively on any subject because she will be able to choose the most convincing reasons to support her claims.

Since the topics are *common* modes of reasoning, almost any audience will understand them. You can use the common topics to argue for or against anything, and you can use them to convince just about anyone. To illustrate, we will explain each topic, model a few arguments, and then give general advice about how to use such reasons.

Induction

Induction abstracts a general pattern from a specific example. Here are a few arguments from induction:

- Legalizing medical marijuana in California resulted in quack doctors and sham dispensaries giving and filling prescriptions to anyone who asked. From this experience we can conclude that, wherever and however a state legalizes medical marijuana, in effect that state also legalizes recreational marijuana.
- The Affordable Care Act eliminated the private healthcare plan that Marti Ceraso had purchased for years, requiring that he buy a more expensive plan featuring services he will never use. So it becomes clear that the Affordable Care Act does not let people keep the health insurance that they had before the law was passed.
- Toll road 183A did not reduce traffic congestion between Cedar Park and Austin, though it did allow private contractors to make a lot of money building roads and charging motorists. Obviously toll roads in Texas are a scam that benefits contractors and impoverishes commuters.

Every one of these arguments, of course, will be more convincing if built on more than one example. One toll road that fails to deliver on its promises may suggest that all toll roads are a scam. Many toll roads that fail to deliver on their promises confirm that toll roads are a scam.

Our first bit of advice, therefore, about arguing from induction is: Don't settle for one example to prove a pattern. Here are a few additional pointers:

Start with the general pattern, and *then* look for the examples. When arguing from induction, you will need to find an example, and that requires some research. But you must also invent a general pattern that you can derive from this example. In fact, when inventing arguments from induction, we recommend that you begin with the general pattern. Then look for an example or several examples to demonstrate specific instances of this pattern. Choose your examples based on how you think they will appeal to the audience. If you want to prove that animals are abused by the beef industry, then you might begin with the most graphic butchering that you can find to move your audience's emotions. Then you could offer a series of shorter and less gruesome examples to show that this one graphic instance is part of a much larger pattern. If you want to prove that charter schools help children from impoverished areas succeed, then you might begin with an extended description of one kid who pulled himself out of poverty in part because of his education at Magnet High. Such an example would be vivid and emotionally moving. It would also grab the audience's attention. Then you could follow with statistics (many examples) of kids who earn more money or achieve higher levels of education than their parents after having attended charter schools.

Pair your argument from induction with an argument at another topic. Disagreements that feature inductive argumentation often devolve into opposing sets of examples. Think of pollsters from opposing political parties during an election cycle: One offers a survey (many examples of people saying something) to show that the country favors Republicans; another offers a different survey (many examples of people saying something else) to show that the country favors Democrats. When you know that counterexamples will oppose your argument, think about switching to another topic of argumentation. Any topic discussed in this book or elsewhere should work. As long as you keep focused on the same subject, your audience won't be confused by a change in argumentative strategy.

Qualify your argument by acknowledging that the general pattern doesn't always hold. Induction doesn't have to prove that specific instances always fit the general pattern. As we like to say, there are always exceptions to the rule. And an argument at the topic of induction can allow and admit to these exceptions. Some kids from impoverished neighborhoods do not get college degrees after attending Magnet High. Some cattle do not spend their lives confined to a small pen before getting bludgeoned to death with a rubber mallet. Counterexamples always exist. Your opponents will quickly find them. Nonetheless, enough kids succeed and enough cows suffer to show that a pattern exists.

As our discussion so far suggests, arguments from induction can give your audience reason to trust, reason to feel, and reason to believe. The audience will trust a speaker who can mention many examples and who can draw general patterns from these examples. Such a person seems knowledgeable and intelligent. An audience will feel various emotions based on the examples placed before them. These feelings will transfer to the general pattern. If we feel disgusted by one instance of poor sanitation in a fast-food restaurant, then we will likely feel disgust toward the entire industry once we think this one instance is part of a broader pattern. Finally, the general conclusion drawn from the specific example or examples is itself a reason to believe. Once we believe that the food processing industry abuses animals, we'll be more likely to conclude that the industry is morally reprehensible and needs strict regulation.

Analogy

Analogies compare two things. You're probably familiar with this common exercise, often repeated on standardized tests: a screwdriver is to a screw as a _____ is to a nail. To complete the analogy, you must figure out the relationship implied by the first two items. Knowing that relationship will help you to figure out the second part of the analogy. The obvious answer to our puzzle is "hammer." Screwdrivers turn screws, and hammers pound nails. Analogical arguments similarly compare things based on some common feature. Analogies don't have to be perfect. In fact, an analogy can work even if the comparison is strained. Think of how many times people say that relearning a skill or a subject is "like riding a bicycle." We all know that a refresher course in trigonometry is nothing like hopping on a 10-speed, but we accept one point of similarity: You never completely forget something you learned very well.

People use analogical arguments to claim that things should be treated similarly: "Tuna is the chicken of the sea, so you can use tuna in lots of dishes that call for chicken." They also use analogical arguments to ask us to feel the same way about different things: "Country and western music is just like gangster rap. Both genres glorify violence, murder, and misogyny. If gangster rap is to blame for urban crime, then country and western music is to blame for every instance of rural domestic violence, every convenience-store robbery, and every bar fight in West Texas." People use analogical arguments to suggest that similar situations will have similar outcomes: "A handful of dedicated leaders and citizens pushed the U.S. government to end segregation. They did it with sit-ins, with marches, with protests, and eventually with legislation. Today a handful of dedicated activists can end abortion-on-demand. We will march to Washington. We will protest outside the offices of legislators. And, to protect the health of the mothers and the lives of the unborn, we will demand laws that restrict abortion services." Like induction, analogy can be quite useful. And like inductions, analogies typically require some research since a good analogy requires a good example.

Like inventing an argument at the topic of induction, inventing an analogy starts with thinking about the conclusion. What do you want your audience to feel or believe? Based on the desired conclusion, you should look for a comparable situation that will elicit similar beliefs or feelings. If you want your audience to believe that the U.S. should not get involved in the Syrian civil war because such intervention will be endless and ineffective, then you should look for a comparable situation when military intervention dragged on without achieving its promised results. If you want to claim that states should abandon the federal government's Common Core education standards because such standards get in the way of good teaching, then you should look for another instance where federal regulations have interrupted people's local and helpful efforts. If you want to argue that the U.S. war on drugs is more harmful than a policy of legalizing and regulating, then you should look for another instance where strict legal penalties did more harm than tolerance and regulation.

As you think through the possible analogies, keep in mind a few rules of thumb:

Though good analogies don't have to be perfect analogies, convincing analogies often compare things with many similarities. As we mention above, the things you're comparing do not have to be exactly alike or even similar. They only have to share one important quality. Federal educational policy is quite different from federal healthcare laws, but you could argue that the No Child Left Behind Act (NCLB) is analogous to the Affordable Care Act (ACA) since both laws are instances of the federal government intervening in something that should have been left to local control or individual choice. Of course, the strength of this analogy lies in the many similarities between the things compared: both NCLB and ACA are federal laws; both are recent; both have been enforced with mixed success.

Analogies don't have to prove that any general patterns exist. In this regard, analogy is easier than induction. Not all or even most efforts at exerting federal control are like NCLB, but the comparison shows that this law, like another, has the potential to be ineffective and destructive.

Extended analogies should feature two things that resemble one another. Those arguing for the legalization of marijuana like to compare federal laws that prohibit the sale of marijuana to the Eighteenth Amendment, which prohibited the sale or consumption of alcohol. You could elaborate on this analogy for paragraphs or pages because there are so many points of comparison. As you elaborate on these points of similarity, the analogy becomes more extended and more convincing.

Effective analogies should feature things that resonate with the audience. To argue against someone comparing criminalization of marijuana to early-twentieth-century prohibition, you could turn to cocaine for an effective counteranalogy and argue that some legal and seemingly harmless drugs should be made illegal. Once widely consumed and put in common products (such as medicines and soft drinks), cocaine was prohibited by the Harrison Act of 1914. You could argue that, like cocaine, marijuana should be studied before the drug is legalized. But for most people, the cocaine-marijuana analogy probably won't resonate as much as the alcohol-marijuana analogy. Most people familiar with U.S. history know about the Prohibition era. And most adults have direct experience with alcohol. Many have experience with marijuana. Fewer have experience with cocaine. Lack of familiarity makes the cocaine-marijuana analogy seem foreign and less convincing. For an even less resonant analogy, you could compare marijuana to MDMA (a.k.a. "molly" or "XTC"), which was legal in the U.S. until 1985.

Further Discussion: Taking action to reduce carbon emissions is a daunting challenge, one that is often met with complaints that there are no feasible ways to substantially reduce the amount of greenhouse gases that people pump into the atmosphere. To counter those who claim that "it's impossible to substantially reduce carbon emissions," speakers often turn to analogy. At the end of his famous lecture (recorded in the documentary film *An Inconvenient Truth* [2006]) Al Gore notes that people decided to reduce chlorofluorocarbons (CFCs) to stop harming the ozone layer. According to Gore, the worldwide effort to reduce CFCs is analogous to the effort to reduce carbon emissions—both require a global effort, and both are possible. More recently, in an episode of the television series *Cosmos* (Episode 12, "The World Set Free" [2014]), Neil deGrasse Tyson argued that reducing carbon emissions is comparable to the worldwide effort to reduce nuclear weapons—both require a global effort, and both are possible. Which of these analogies will resonate better with a contemporary audience? Which analogy compares things that most closely resemble each other? What would be a counteranalogy, a problem that was indeed too big for everyone to solve together?

Difference

Like analogies, arguments at the topic of difference draw conclusions based on comparisons. Instead of highlighting similarities, however, arguments at the topic of difference focus on differences. In order for analogies to work, the audience must assume that similar things deserve similar responses or will have similar results. In order for an argument at the topic of difference to work, the audience must believe that different things deserve different responses and will have different results:

- If you love capitalism and democracy, you should hate socialism and dictatorship.
- If government regulation kills jobs and stalls growth, then the free market and private industry will kick-start the economy and employ hundreds of thousands of people.
- If Republicans favor individual rights and market freedoms, then Democrats must favor state regulation and government handouts.
- If Republicans favor corporations and the wealthy, then Democrats fight for small businesses and the middle class.

To invent arguments at the topic of difference, begin with your conclusion. What do you want your audience to think, feel, or do? Then try to find or invent something that will lead them to the opposite belief, sentiment, or action.

Like analogies, arguments about difference are more effective if they feature good examples, if they present close comparisons, and if they resonate with the audience. In fact, all the advice we give about analogies applies to arguments at the topic of difference. Except this: While analogies don't have to be perfect to be convincing, arguments at the topic of difference do have to compare completely—or at least extremely—different things. No one will assume that slightly different things deserve very different reactions. No one will believe that nearly identical policies will have wildly variant results.

Analogies and differences can give an audience reasons to believe, to trust, and to feel, so both are versatile topics. But arguments at the topic of difference tend to have more emotional resonance. Analogies can ask the audience to think and to feel the same way about two comparable matters. If I want to convince you that we should pass legislation outlawing discrimination against transgender people, then I can compare such discrimination to early 20th-century segregation. I can say that, like segregation, discrimination against transgender people violates people's rights and liberties. This is essentially a reason to believe that we should support legislation that outlaws discrimination against transgender Americans. But it is also a reason to feel good about the campaign against such discrimination: Since transgender rights are analogous to racial equality, all good feelings about civil rights apply to both. Arguments at the topic of difference work similarly but have much stronger emotional resonance. Furthermore, arguments at the topic of difference don't ask the audience to feel the same emotion about two things. Arguments at the topic of difference ask the audience to feel different emotions but with the same intensity. Arguments that appeal to nationalism often work this way. It is common, for instance, to hear the following reason to feel animosity toward certain corporations and certain individuals: If you love American industry, then you should hate companies that manufacture overseas. Another argument at the topic of difference is commonly used to convince people that they should disdain any opposition to an armed intervention: If you honor our soldiers, then you should despise war protesters.

Correlation

As we've explained so far, certain kinds of arguments call for or depend upon certain kinds of evidence. Analogies, inductions, and arguments at the topic of difference require examples. Arguments about correlation typically depend upon signs. The basic presupposition behind an argument at the topic of correlation is that certain things relate to or somehow go with other things. Since some things tend to go with other things, they are often understood as signs that something else exists or will happen. If you want to prove that someone committed murder in cold blood, then you will have to find things that typically correlate to premeditated murder: "After killing the victim and dumping the body, this heinous man went to a local diner and ordered a grilled cheese sandwich." Since people typically eat when they feel peaceful, it seems reasonable to conclude that this person was not passionate or upset before, during, or especially after the killing.

Correlation is useful when trying to invent reasons to trust (or not to trust) someone and when inventing reasons to believe that something exists or will exist.

Correlation can give an audience reasons to trust an authority or a speaker. Why can you trust this person as a knowledgeable source? She's written three books on the subject, and publication tends to go with erudition. Why should you not trust this person at all? She said the exact opposite thing to someone else last week, and inconsistency often relates to duplicity. You can present such reasons in support of an argument that your audience should trust (or not trust) an authority whom you cite. And you can also present such reasons to convince your audience to trust you. Copious research often correlates with authority. If you show your audience that you have done a lot of research, they will trust you based on this correlation. Living in a community often correlates with goodwill toward the people in that community. If you tell an audience of Texans that you live in Texas (or Austin), they will trust you as someone who bears them goodwill based on this correlation.

Correlation can give an audience reason to believe that something exists or will exist. While it is helpful when trying to invent reasons to trust, correlation also can offer reasons to believe that something exists or is the case. If you want to prove that global climate change is real, you should look for things that accompany warmer climates: increased rainfall, intense storms, drought. If you want to prove that global warming is a theory blown out of proportion by histrionic scientists, then you should look for inconsistencies in their reports or evidence that has been altered or suppressed. Such things tend to go along with conspiracies to misinform. Arguments about motive tend to rely exclusively on the correlation of behavior and inward sentiment. Since we can't see into a person's mind or soul to verify his emotional state, we have to assume that a frown means he's sad and a clenched fist means he's angry. Such expressions relate to inward feelings.

To invent an argument at the topic of correlation, we suggest that you first figure out your claim. What do you want your audience to believe exists or is the case? Then try to think of things that correlate. If you want them to believe that smoking marijuana has harmful mental side effects, try to think of symptoms that correlate to reduced cognition or memory function: slurred speech, lack of ambition, poor short-term recall. If you want your audience to think that a political candidate is trying to win votes by saying things that she does not believe, then look for things that correlate with deception: inconsistency between words and deeds; vague messages that don't commit to any specific actions; continually changing positions over time.

Before we move on to the next topic of argumentation, a brief warning about correlation: Historically, people have drawn questionable conclusions based on things that tend to accompany or relate to other things. We assume that expertise is the same the world over, so we trust meteorologists who pontificate about global warming (even though they are experts about weather, not climate), and we trust stock traders who talk about economics (even though they are experts about equities markets, not national or global economies). Correlation also leads people to assume causation, even though there may be no evidence that two things often found together cause one another. Stable marriages and financial well-being tend to go together. But we don't know which (if either) causes the other. Anyone who recommends that others get or stay married so that they can be financially stable is mistaking correlation for causation. Much medical science is dedicated to separating correlation (symptoms) from causation (disease). In public argument, we tend to be less exact than medical doctors, but we should nevertheless be careful. Most worrisome is that correlation has contributed to regrettable developments in recent history. All racial profiling is based on correlation of skin color and criminality. Much discrimination is based on correlation of inferior social standing and gender or ethnicity.

While you should be careful with correlation, you should not rule it out as an argumentative tool. In fact, despite

Further Discussion: Much contemporary advertising ("image" ads, for instance) depend upon correlation of a lifestyle and a product. Since successful athletes and a brand of shoe go together, then you should buy that shoe. Since attractive people and a kind of beer go together, you should drink that beer. Is it insulting to suggest that lifestyles and identities correlate with products? Are marketers really telling us that we can be cool if we buy the right soda? Or are they simply showing us the relations that already exist between social groups and brand names?

its dangers, this topic of argumentation persists because it is reasonable to assume that some things relate to or tend to go with other things. Rain doesn't cause thunder, or vice versa, but the two regularly go together. And the person who hears a low rumbling in the distant sky and refuses to take out an umbrella because there is no guaranteed causal connection between the discharge of static electrical charges and precipitation is a wet fool.

Definition

Definition, along with induction, is among the most common kinds of argument. Definitions give people reasons to believe certain things. When you hear a news anchor describe an area hit by tornadoes as a "federal disaster area," you believe that the damage is severe. You imagine homes torn from their foundations, cars turned over, people injured or dead. Definitions give us reasons to feel a certain way. "Federal disaster areas" warrant our concern and our desire to help. Finally, definitions tell us what to do. We should give federal money and offer private charity to a "federal disaster area," so people can rebuild their homes and recover their losses. Every definition presents some belief, evokes some feeling, and suggests some action. To call someone's unfortunate demise an "accidental death" is to ask the audience to believe that no one is to blame, so they should feel sorrow and offer consolation. To call that same person's death a "homicide" is to tell the audience that someone is to blame, so they should feel angry and find the culprit.

Because definitions are such powerful and useful arguments, they often sit at the center of controversies. Different stakeholders can be identified, as we mentioned in the introductory chapters, by the definitions that they prefer. If you are pro-life, then you define abortion as "murder," and you define the contents of a mother's womb as a "baby." If you are pro-choice, you prefer different definitions, such as "medical procedure" and "fetus." If you favor immigration reform, then you will define people who do not have explicit permission from the federal government to live and work in the U.S. as "undocumented immigrants." If you prefer to keep the immigration laws as they are (or to make their enforcement more strict), then you will define these same people as "illegals." If you favor a tax on inheritances valued at more than 5.3 million dollars, then you will likely call it an "estate tax." If you want to reduce or eliminate such a levy, then you will likely call it a "death tax."

Contemporary professionals who advise politicians and run election campaigns spend a lot of their time worrying about definitions because they know that the party or the politician who invents a new definition will guide emotions and policy for a long time. Think of how different U.S. history would be if we had decided to define the attacks on September 11, 2001, as "international crimes" rather than as "acts of terrorism." (At the time, many argued unsuccessfully for such a definition.) Think of how different law enforcement would be today if we defined every mass shooting as an incidence of "terrorism." In order to invent definitional arguments, we suggest that you begin with the thing you want to define. Then ask yourself, "What do I want the audience to believe, to think, and to do about this thing?" Finally, try to find terms that will lead the audience to believe, think, and do as you wish. If you want people to believe that college admissions policies favor certain applicants based on race regardless of academic excellence, then you should look for words that suggest such a quality: "race-based admissions." If you want the audience to feel that college admissions policies attending to academic excellence are fair, then you should look for words that suggest justice: "merit-based admissions." If you want your audience to eliminate admissions policies that consider race, then you should look for words that suggest illegality: "unconstitutional race-based admissions policies." If you prefer, on the other hand, that your audience appreciate and maintain college admissions policies that consider race, then you should look for another definition: "college admissions programs that promote diversity."

To help you invent and elaborate your definition arguments, we offer three pointers: (1) Explain the category; (2) identify the essence; (3) emphasize the effect.

Explaining the definitional category: Many definition arguments ask the audience to put something specific into a broader group of other, similar things. To say that race-based admissions policies are "unconstitutional," for instance, is to say that these policies belong in the broad category of unconstitutional things. All the things in this category will share certain features, just like all mammals have hair and give birth to live young (to name two shared traits). If you can explain the category and show your audience what qualities constitute the category, then you can also show your audience why this particular object belongs in the category. Mammals have hair, give birth to live young, and produce milk. Mice have hair, give birth to live young, and produce milk. Therefore mice are mammals. Unconstitutional policies do not accord with some part of the U.S. Constitution in effect or in practice. Someone might argue that race-based admissions policies result in a quota system, which in effect violates the Fourteenth Amendment of the U.S. Constitution, so they are unconstitutional. Often, people will disagree about the category itself. In these cases, you must explain the category before defining the object. The word "fair" carries so many definitions that few efforts to define something as "fair" can get away without explaining what is meant by this category. But even when there is no disagreement about the category—even when everyone agrees about what "terrorism," "unconstitutional," or "democratic" means—defining the category can give someone an advantage because that definition might become the standard that everyone will use.

Identify the definitional essence: Like explaining the category, identifying the essence of a definition allows you to set the terms of the debate. Explaining the category typically requires that you describe several qualities and then show that your object exhibits these qualities. Mammals, as we mention above, have hair, give birth to live young, and produce milk. If an animal does not have all of these qualities (and several others), it's not a mammal. (The duck-billed platypus complicates this definition, of course: It's a rare egg-laying mammal, a monotreme.) Things get messier when trying to deal with contested categories. We all agree about what qualities make a mammal, but what qualities make a democracy? Popular elections? Representation by a body of legislators? Direct ballot initiatives? Suffrage for all citizens? Or all of the above? If you choose all of the above, then you might be surprised to learn that you don't live in a democratic state, for Texas's state constitution doesn't allow direct ballot initiatives. Many cities, such as Austin, do allow them, however. Not surprisingly, there is much debate among Texas residents about whether the state government, in order to be truly democratic, should allow direct ballot initiatives.

Identifying the definitional essence cuts through all the complexity by asserting that one quality is at the heart of the category. A democracy is any government that gives sovereignty to the people. Popular sovereignty, therefore, is the essence of democracy. The other qualities are inessential. Historically, arguments about Christianity have waffled between those who explain and those who essentialize the category of "true Christian." Theologians who insist on a robust catechism claim that in order to be a Christian, one must believe in many things, such as the coeval existence of three figures in the godhead, the impending return of Christ to judge the living and the dead, the literal historical truth of the creation narrative in the book of Genesis. Theologians arguing for a minimal catechism claim that one belief constitutes the essence of Christianity: acceptance of Jesus Christ as humankind's savior. We oversimplify millennia of theological arguments to make a simple point: Identifying the essence of the definitional category can effectively counter an argument that explains the definitional category.

Emphasize the definition's effect: As you've noticed by now, definitional debates quickly become abstract and complicated. Much of Western philosophy and law is filled with such endless arguments about how to define "good," "nature," "humanity," and "property." At a certain point, people stop talking about the things themselves and talk exclusively about the categories. They argue about words and their meanings. Such disagreements tend to be irreconcilable. In the abortion debate, for instance, the effort to define "life" has led to legal abstractions and confusions that few can parse. The U.S. Supreme Court ultimately decided to avoid defining "life" but to define "viable" as "potentially able to live outside the mother's womb." Any other definition or term would risk effects that the Court did not desire. Defining "life" more fully or more strictly would impinge on the mother's right to privacy and impose on a doctor's right to practice medicine. Rather than focusing on the essence or the explanation of the category, the Court's definition focuses on the effects. Many *functional* definitions exist because we like the effects that they have. If we expand the definition of "historical landmark" to include architecturally interesting though fairly recent buildings, then we can preserve buildings that we like even if they're not that old. If we define a "national monument" as any protected area, then the president of the United States can prevent the destruction of natural formations without asking for congressional approval. We allow such definitions not because we think that "protection" is an essential quality of monuments. In fact, when most people think of monuments, they think of marble statues in Washington, D.C., not rock formations in Wyoming. But the definition convinces because the audience likes its effects.

Emphasizing the definition's effects is an effective way to step into a longstanding and complicated argument that has already featured many explanations and essentializations. After a while, when the audience is tired of trying to see all the necessary qualities or to see into the essence of the matter, they just want a definition that does something good. In this circumstance, a definition that emphasizes its effect is welcome.

Causation

To argue at the topic of causation, you must assert that something causes or is the effect of something else. Causal arguments rarely stand alone. Only in select controversies do people argue heatedly and exclusively about whether one thing causes another thing. More typically, speakers use causal arguments to convince the audience of something else. For example, if you want to make someone dislike an action, then you can show that it is the effect of a bad motive or that it is the cause of someone else's suffering. I am happy that John paid for my dinner last night—until you point out that he only bought me dinner because he wants to butter me up before asking me for a loan. You feel good about your new diamond necklace until I point out that purchasing diamond jewelry indirectly supports gangs of armed thugs who terrorize parts of Africa so that they can maintain control of the diamond market. Causal arguments are also useful when trying to convince people to do (or not do) something. Children don't like to eat vegetables, so we tell them that eating carrots will improve their eyesight. Adults like to eat cake until they are reminded that a moment on the lips is a lifetime on the hips.

Causal arguments are easy to make, but they're hard to prove. Speakers often rely on some common assumption about what kinds of things cause or result from other kinds of things. Since we typically assume that eating sweets causes weight gain, we will readily accept your argument that cake will make us heavy. We don't readily associate eating habits with disease, so we will less readily accept an argument that eating cake will make us diabetic. A consistent sequence of

Brief Exercise, *Dissoi Logoi*:
To create persuasive definition arguments, sometimes the best strategy is to experiment with each of the techniques outlined above until you discover the form of argumentation your intended audience is most likely to accept. One way of doing so is to practice writing *dissoi logoi* ("double arguments"). Invent arguments for and against several propositions. As a class, see if you can elaborate on the following propositions: "Allowing doctors to prescribe lethal amounts or combinations of narcotics to terminally ill patients is *euthanasia*" and "allowing doctors to prescribe lethal amounts or combinations of narcotics to terminally ill patients is *physician-assisted suicide*." Skilled speakers can persuasively argue both of these propositions without sacrificing their actual positions. The trick is recognizing how and when to shift from one definitional strategy to another.

events can also serve as evidence of causation. If you consistently get a rash after you use a certain sunscreen, then it's reasonable to conclude that the sunscreen causes skin irritation. Finally, correlation can be used to establish causation. Things that consistently go together often (but certainly not always) are in a causal relationship with one another. Since the children whose parents read to them consistently do well in school, we assume that reading to kids before bedtime will boost their academic performance. All such arguments about causation are imperfect, to say the least. Moreover, because causal arguments are so hard to prove, they tend to drag on. A fairly intuitive connection between contact sports and mental dysfunction is only now under debate because it has been so hard for scientists to conclusively prove that repeated blows to the head—even when a person wears a helmet and does not suffer from an evident concussion—can lead to long-term emotional and cognitive problems. Thankfully, in order to be convincing, arguments about causation do not have to be conclusive. The final scientific verdict may still be unsettled, but we can see enough correlation and sequence to know that we must start reducing the amount of head trauma that occurs in popular sports.

Using the Topics

We've reviewed a range of argumentative topics to get you started. There are others. In fact, for thousands of years rhetoric instructors have told students to invent lots of arguments at numerous topics. Unfortunately, knowing the difference between an argument at the topic of correlation and an argument at the topic of causation won't make you more persuasive. To use these topics well, you have to practice. Write down your principal claim—the idea, feeling, or action that you want your audience to believe, experience, or do. Then go down the list of topics. Try to invent at least one argument at each topic to support your principal claim. Inventing more than one reason at each topic is even better still. Some of the topics will lead you to useful reasons. Some won't lead you to any reasons. But some topics will lead you to arguments you would not have considered. And a few topics will lead you to very persuasive reasons. The goal of this exercise (and of this chapter) is to invent more than you can use. Then you can decide which arguments are the best. The topics should help you to find more things to say. Arguing at the topic of correlation, we'll point out that the speaker with more things to say often has better things to say. Arguing at the topic of causation, we'll notice that having better things to say typically results in a winning argument.

Short Writing Assignment: One of the most popular exercises assigned to students of rhetoric required that they argue both sides of a contentious issue. In ancient Greek it was called the *antilogiai* ("opposing arguments"), and in Latin *argumentum in utramque partem* ("argument against both sides"). The topics played a key role in this exercise, for they offered students a way to argue contrasting opinions using the same basic argumentative moves. Using the six topics in this chapter, write one- or two-sentence arguments on both sides of a case. Use our example as a guide:

Principal Claim: *Tipping in restaurants should persist as the principal way to reward good service.*	**Principal Claim:** *Tipping in restaurants should be replaced with another way to reward good service.*
Induction: Tipping guarantees that good service continues. At the Crown and Anchor, two bartenders were given different tips because they offered different qualities of service. When the lower-paid server saw how much more he could earn by being nicer and more attentive, he started to do a better job..	**Induction:** Servers prefer to collect a guaranteed salary, especially if it comes with benefits, because they know that they will earn less if they have to scrounge for tips. At the Black Star Co-op, when given the choice, servers elected to receive a salary with benefits.
Analogy: Tipping for good table service is like giving an end-of-year bonus for good sales. Both promote initiative.	**Analogy:** Tipping for good table service is like letting students decide teachers' salaries. Both allow cruel punishment for questionable reasons.
Difference: At the post office, where people know they're going to get a check no matter when your mail arrives, workers are slow, unenthusiastic, and rarely helpful. Tipping, on the other hand, motivates people to work hard for every customer.	**Difference:** At Starbucks, where employees are given job security and benefits, they work hard because they feel like they're part of a team, and they don't have to always worry about whether being underpaid for the next latte will leave them unable to pay the rent. Tipping, on the other hand, leaves servers uncertain and bitter, so they often work less or have terrible attitudes.
Correlation: : Merit-based rewards and high performance are often found in the same organizations. Tipping and good service go together.	**Correlation:** Service industries that pay their workers with tips are more likely to have employees living below the poverty line. Tipping and poverty go together.
Definition: Fair evaluation of service should be based on customer satisfaction. Since tipping is the best expression of a customer's evaluation of the service, it is the fairest way to compensate restaurant servers.	**Definition:** Unfair treatment in the workplace happens anytime workers are evaluated based on customer whim rather than on an honest measure of their performance. Tipping is therefore unfair.
Causation: Tipping leads to good service, well-paid servers, and a vibrant restaurant industry.	**Causation:** Tipping leads to wage theft, poverty, and a stressful work environment.

CHAPTER 9

Concession, Refutation, and Rebuttal

ootball coaches like to repeat the maxim, "The best defense is a good offense." By this, of course, they mean that the best way to defend against opponents who score touchdowns is to score touchdowns yourself. We can say something similar, though reversed, about argumentation: The most convincing argument is a good counterargument. In Chapter 8, we offer advice about inventing arguments. Invention is argumentative offense, coming up with reasons to convince your audience. In this chapter, we teach you argumentative defense. You will invent counterarguments to show your audience that other viewpoints aren't as convincing as yours. The best argument is a good counterargument because it's difficult to convince an audience that knows the opposing viewpoints. As the audience listens to the argument, they'll wonder, "What about those who disagree? Don't they have good evidence and persuasive reasons? Why should I accept your viewpoint over theirs?" The slightest doubt will stall persuasion, even if you make a convincing case.

Before we teach you how to invent counterarguments, allow us to explain *why* you should learn to invent counterarguments. To begin with, as we explain above, countering the opposition has a strategic value. If you can show your audience that your viewpoint is not *just* persuasive but the *most* persuasive, then you will have a better chance at convincing them.

Furthermore, countering the opposition also has a practical value. If you can build an argument that fairly represents and counters your opponents' arguments, then you will likely make the best argument possible. When you refuse to acknowledge or address other viewpoints, you miss the opportunity to improve by honestly debating. Here's an analogy to prove our claim: A boxer who never steps into the ring is not as good as one who spars regularly. And a speaker who never addresses an opposing viewpoint is not as good as a seasoned debater.

Finally, countering the opposition has ethical value. To prove this claim, we offer a causal argument: Fairly representing yet refuting others leads to disagreement without disagreeable behavior. To have productive public disagreement, people must defend their viewpoints without alienating those who think differently. When we argue without upsetting one another, we ensure that the conversation will continue. When we dispute without enraging one another, we keep dissent from turning into violence. Current political debate features many people who disagree *while being* disagreeable, to the detriment of citizens and public debate.

Choosing a Good Opponent

The first step toward writing a good refutation is choosing a good opponent. Once your audience sees that you've chosen to counter a reasonable and persuasive opponent, they will think more highly of you. Speakers who pick on flimsy or foolish claims are bullying the weak. But bullies don't challenge the strong. When you choose a good opponent, you give your audience a reason to trust you as an intelligent, informed, and capable speaker. If you can counter a worthy opponent, you must be worthy of respect yourself.

The next step toward writing a good counterargument is to represent the opposing argument fairly. It's common to find speakers unfairly representing those who think differently. Such unfair or oversimplified representation is called making a *straw person* out of your opposition. You're not contending with a real, flesh-and-blood adversary. Rather, you're fighting a dummy that's much easier to defeat. If your audience knows the opposition or their viewpoints, then your straw-person representation will look duplicitous, and you will look untrustworthy. Furthermore, your straw-person representation will poison the conversation. No one will want to read your argument or speak with you because no one will want to be misrepresented. For all these reasons, we encourage you to pick a good opponent, someone you find convincing, even someone difficult to completely disagree with. Fairly represent the opposing viewpoint without simplifying or distorting. Then make your best effort at showing why this viewpoint is not as persuasive as yours. If you have questions about how to represent your opposition fairly, we encourage you to revisit Chapter 2 of this textbook. Everything we say about fairly summarizing sources applies to fairly representing your argumentative antagonist.

Conceding to Good Arguments

If you pick the best opposing viewpoint, then you may find yourself unable to refute everything your rival says. You may even find yourself agreeing with some of your rival's reasons, even as you disagree with his principal claim. But just because you can't counter every bit of evidence and every reason does not mean you've lost the argument. In fact, you can make your argument more persuasive by admitting that you agree with some of your opponent's claims, some of his evidence, even a few of his reasons. This is called *concession*: the willing and open admission that you cannot or do not want to argue about certain things. Too much concession will make it seem like you don't disagree at all. But confessing that you agree somewhat with your opponent will give your audience reason to trust you as a reasonable person who doesn't throw out good ideas.

The trouble with concession, as we've mentioned, is that it can make your position seem weak. The audience might think, "Why should we believe this speaker if she

Brief Exercise, Rearticulating Claims: Write down all of the claims you want to make for your next argument. Then ask one of your classmates (or your roommate, or anyone else) to help you clarify your claims by rearticulating them until you are satisfied that the way they say it is the way you meant it.

Here's an example:

> **Claim of student 1:** People should eat only organic food because it is always better for their health and for the environment.
> **Student 2:** So are you saying that *all* people should eat only organic food because it's better for their health and for the environment?
> **S1:** Yes.
> **S2:** Okay, if I understand you, even people who cannot afford organic food should eat only organic food because it is better to starve in a developing country than to eat nonorganic food.
> **S1:** No, that's not what I'm saying. Let me try again. People in the United States who can afford organic food should eat only organic food because it is better for their health and for the environment.
> **S2:** Okay, so what you're saying is that if people can afford to eat organic food, they should eat only organic food because it is always healthier and better for the environment, even if it takes lots of fossil fuels to transport it to your supermarket.
> **S1:** No, that's not what I meant. What I was trying to say was that if you can afford it, organic food produced locally in the U.S. is better for your health and the environment than nonorganic food.
> **S2:** So it sounds to me like what you are claiming is that if Americans can afford it, they should buy locally grown organic food because it's better for their health and for the environment.
> **S1:** Yes, that is what I'm claiming.

You can use this same technique to scrutinize the opposition's claims. Not only will doing so help you to clarify what the opposition is claiming, but it also may help you discover places where you can reasonably challenge parts of that opposing claim.

keeps admitting that her opponent is right all the time? Why not believe her opponent instead?" To prevent this reaction, we suggest a few common tactics:

- *Explain that the points to which you've conceded don't matter.* This strategy requires that you show why your concession in no way undercuts your argument. For instance: "Climatologists have shown that the earth is getting warmer. I cannot deny that. But just because the earth is getting warmer doesn't mean that people are the primary cause. Nor do climate scientists' conclusions about increasing temperatures prove that we can reduce carbon emissions without crippling the economy."
- *Explain that the points to which you've conceded actually support your argument.* This strategy requires that you turn your concession into a reason or a bit of evidence

to support your principal claim. For instance: "Jennings admits that changing eligibility requirements for Medicaid will boost enrollment. He's right: More people will have healthcare if we expand Medicaid. But, if we expand Medicaid, then more people will depend on government-funded healthcare. That's exactly why we cannot change the eligibility requirements for Medicaid. We need to wean people off government support."

- *Explain that the concessions form a common ground on which you can build a new consensus.* This strategy is especially effective when writing to an audience that already agrees with your opponent. By showing the audience that you also agree with your opponent but that you arrive at different conclusions, you can convince your audience that they can also agree about the common ground while disagreeing about the conclusion. For instance: "Since, as we agree, the university shouldn't impose its secular version of diversity on any religious organization, the university should not sponsor any Christian student organization. The freedom to meet, worship, and believe will be protected. The university cannot impose secular beliefs or practices on religious organizations as long as they remain voluntary societies supported by member contributions and not university resources."

Refuting the Evidence

While concession is a powerful tool, sometimes you want to simply refute your opponent's argument. Moreover, concession and refutation can work together. You can admit that some of your opponent's arguments have merit while showing that others are simply wrong. The most common strategy for refuting the opposition is to counter the evidence. The analytic tools we present in Chapter 4 will help you to identify the evidence in an argument. Once you've located your opponent's key pieces of evidence, you can counter in a number of ways. Here are just a few:

- *Offer counterevidence of exactly the same kind.* This strategy pits one example against another, one bit of testimony against another, one maxim against its opposite. For instance: "Lu says that the example of his grandparents' successful long-distance relationship proves that absence makes the heart grow fonder. Jenny and Geraldine's struggle to stay together while living in different countries proves something very different: out of sight, out of mind."
- *Present a different kind of evidence that leads to a different conclusion.* This strategy aims to shift the debate away from the evidence that favors your opponent's conclusions. For instance: "Silverman piles up the statistics about income inequality and social mobility to show that poor people in America cannot expect better lives than those their parents enjoyed. All these numbers, however, seem hollow when we hear Joaquin Castañeda tell his story of growing up in East Austin, learning to cook, and ultimately starting his own successful restaurant chain."
- *Question the quality or the source of the evidence.* This strategy gives the audience a reason not to trust the information or the speaker. "When we look closely at Republican examples of people hurt by the Affordable Care Act, we see people who claim that they can't find affordable healthcare but who haven't really looked for it.

When we ask detailed questions, we learn that few policies were canceled this year, and the people whose premiums increased will pay a little more money for much better healthcare."

Refuting the Inference

Refuting evidence counters your opponent's arguments. But, as we point out in Chapter 6, sometimes an argument relies mostly or entirely on reasons that people invent. In these cases, you must address the inference—the manner of reasoning—rather than the evidence.

Nowadays, students often learn to refute inferences by studying *argumentative fallacies*, under the assumption that certain kinds of arguments are always wrong (i.e., fallacious), regardless of the audience or situation. Such arguments can never be trusted because they're logically flawed. We prefer to avoid the term *fallacy*, however, because it suggests something that we know isn't true. You can't decide how persuasive an argument will be without considering the situation and the audience. Since most arguments can convince some people, no argument is *rhetorically fallacious*, though many arguments are *rhetorically flawed*. All of the topics that we discuss in Chapter 8 can lead either to rhetorically persuasive or rhetorically flawed arguments.

Before we get into the specific types of flawed arguments, allow us to demonstrate the difference between a reasonable and a flawed inference with a brief example. Refutations often conclude that an argument is wrong because the speaker cannot be trusted. The flawed version of this inference is called an *ad hominem* argument (*ad hominem* means "with respect to the person" in Latin). An *ad hominem* argument inappropriately attacks the speaker's credibility. But as we've noted at several points, questioning and attacking a speaker's credibility is often entirely appropriate. Imagine that a speaker makes an argument about the effects of late-term abortion on a mother's health, claiming that we should believe him based on his credentials as a doctor. In this case, it would be wholly reasonable and appropriate to point out that the speaker is not a gynecologist (a doctor who specializes in women's reproductive health) but instead an ophthalmologist (a doctor who specializes in eye care). And we shouldn't trust what an ophthalmologist says about women's reproductive health. In this case, the argument is premised on the speaker's authority. If the speaker's authority is not acceptable, then the argument is not reasonable. The audience might not think it appropriate, on the other hand, to question the speaker's authority because he cheated on his wife. According to such an audience, marital fidelity does not make anyone a qualified medical professional, so it's irrelevant to the argument about abortion and women's health.

Our point is that the same inference (deciding not to believe an argument because you don't trust the speaker) can be either persuasive or flawed. Only the audience can decide what they will accept as a reasonable conclusion and what they will dismiss as a flawed inference. Knowing the difference between the reasonable and the flawed versions of each argument will help you to invent refutations. But you must not forget the audience, for, ultimately, the audience will distinguish between an *ad hominem* argument and an appropriate attack on someone's credibility. Below we explore other flawed versions of common argumentative topics. We encourage you to review them. When you are reading your opponent's arguments, try to identify the topics used, and ask yourself, "Can I convince my audience that my opponent offers a flawed argument rather than a reasonable inference?"

Overgeneralization

Overgeneralization is the flawed version of the argument at the topic of induction. When an audience refuses to abstract a pattern based on an example or a group of examples, they feel that the speaker too quickly jumps to a general conclusion. For example, if an audience has known many people who have overcome poverty, then they will be skeptical of a statistical study claiming that people generally have little social mobility in the U.S. And similarly, if the audience is familiar with the statistical study demonstrating that few people escape poverty, they will refuse to conclude that social mobility is common based on a few anecdotes about people who pull themselves up by their bootstraps. Both skeptical audiences will call these arguments "overgeneralizations."

Saying that your opponent's argument is an overgeneralization will not refute the claim. You will have to prove that your opponent overgeneralizes. You can do this in a number of ways:

- *Show an exception to the rule.* If, in one important instance, the pattern doesn't hold, then the generalization may not be warranted.
- *Show another contradictory pattern.* Your audience will doubt the pattern asserted by your opponent if you can show them the exact opposite pattern.
- *Show how many possible examples there are.* If your audience sees that your opponent relies upon one or even one hundred examples, but the number of possible examples is much larger (one thousand or one hundred thousand), then they will wonder if such a small sample should lead them to a general conclusion about such a large group.
- *Show that the examples chosen by your opponent are not representative.* If an argument at the topic of induction relies upon examples that are notably different from what your audience commonly sees, then they will not draw general conclusions based on your opponent's peculiar examples.

False Analogy

False analogy is the flawed version of an argument at the topic of analogy. An analogy will seem false to an audience who believe that two things do not sufficiently resemble one another to warrant a comparison. Often, an audience's familiarity with one of the elements in an analogy will interrupt their willingness to accept the comparison. For example, an audience that is very familiar with the Watergate scandal (because of having studied American history or having lived during the 1960s) may refuse to accept any comparison to a recent congressional investigation. Such an audience will quickly point out all the differences: "Watergate involved criminal activity that a sitting president knew about, sanctioned, and then tried to cover up. When responding to the attack on the U.S. embassy in Benghazi, Secretary of State Hillary Clinton did not break any laws or cover up any wrongdoing." Therefore, you probably won't convince this audience to use the term, "Benghazi-gate." They will think the analogy is hopelessly false.

When trying to refute your opponent's arguments at the topic of analogy, you should point out all the differences between the things being compared. Even if you concede that the two things are similar in the important ways that your opponent contends, you can still call the analogy into question by pointing to all the differences. To return to our earlier example, the man skeptical of the Watergate-Benghazi analogy may say, "Nixon changed his story about what happened at the Watergate hotel, just as Secretary Clinton changed her mind about whether to call the attack on the Benghazi embassy an act of 'terror.' But the similarities end there. Nixon's campaign organization paid men to break into a hotel room and steal information from the Democratic National Committee. Then Nixon broke the law by destroying evidence that would tie the Watergate burglary to him. Clinton didn't break any laws, nor did she destroy any evidence to cover her activities."

Faulty Comparison
Faulty comparison is a flawed version of the argument at the topic of difference. An audience refusing to see the differences will also refuse to accept the speaker's comparison. Such an audience will retort that a more thorough comparison will reveal that these two things are not so different after all. And if these things are not so different after all, then they do not merit opposite reactions. To refute an argument at the topic of difference, you should point out all the similarities between the two things being compared. Imagine, for instance, that your opponent has claimed that European-style socialism has led to generous welfare programs, massive public debt, and a stagnant economy. On the other hand, American-style capitalism has led to small government, little deficit spending, and a vibrant economy. Therefore, we should pursue American-style capitalism by cutting unemployment benefits. You can point out the similarities between U.S. and European economic policies: Many European countries, like the U.S., have public welfare, public retirement, and public healthcare systems in place. Many European countries carry as much or even less public debt per capita than the U.S. And the European economy, in recent years, has experienced only slightly less growth than the U.S. economy. If the two economies are not that different, then we shouldn't cut public benefits to avoid "European-style socialism." After all, European-style socialism and American-style capitalism look a lot alike and have similar results.

Mistaking Correlation for Causation
Mistaking correlation for causation is the flawed version of the argument at the topic of correlation. The sports fanatic mistakes correlation for causation when insisting that the Longhorns' success depends on his game-day attire because the UT football team wins every time he wears his lucky jersey. Superstitions, we can all admit, are silly. But very serious arguments persisting for many years have been similarly flawed. For centuries,

people believed that bad smells caused disease when, in fact, bad smells simply accompany widespread sickness and death. During centuries-past, European plague epidemics, people wore fragrant flowers ("a pocket full of posies") to keep themselves from catching a deadly ailment whose first symptom was a circular red sore ("a ring around the rosie").

The best way to refute an argument at the topic of correlation is to give evidence showing that another cause can be tied directly to this effect. We have seen the plague bacterium under microscopes; we know that fleas who live on rats carry the bacterium in their guts; we can scientifically verify that such fleas infect people. But sometimes, such irrefutable evidence is not available. If you don't have irrefutable evidence of causation to challenge a claim at the topic of correlation, then you will have to give your audience reasons to doubt the supposed causal connection. You can do this in a number of ways:

- *Point out that there are other, equally plausible causes.* How does your friend know it's *his* jersey causing the Longhorns to win? Maybe *your* gym socks are really the cause. Or maybe it's the new head coach.
- *Note that sometimes the effect appears without the presumed cause.* If your friend's jersey causes the Longhorns to win, then why did they lose last week? And why were they losing during the first half of the game two weeks ago, only to win in overtime? Did he take his jersey off for the first half of the game?
- *Explain that there's no reason for these things to cause one another, so the more likely explanation is coincidence.* How on earth could wearing a dingy football jersey in a cramped college apartment affect the outcome of a football game hundreds of miles away?

Essentialization

Essentialization is a flawed version of argumentation at the topic of definition. When a speaker essentializes, she assumes that her definition captures the most important qualities (the essence) of something. An anthropologist familiar with the variety of human cultures and beliefs will think that the following definition essentializes humankind: People are rational animals. Our skeptical anthropologist will demand, "What do you mean by 'rational'?" She might add, "I've seen plenty of people who don't know what a syllogism is and who can't manage complicated arithmetic, but they're no less 'people' because they lack this essential quality." Since definitions always focus on certain qualities (or on a single quality), they always run the risk of essentializing. And essentializing definitions always run the risk of excluding or deriding someone or something. Once you define people as "rational animals," you have to say all those nonrational, bipedal hominids are not people. And if they're not people, they don't deserve to be treated as people. Definitions excluding some from the category of *people* have apologized for slavery, invasion, and genocide. But essentializing definitions also run the risk of inappropriately admitting something or someone into a category. Once you define *democracy* as "any government built upon popular sovereignty," then you have to accept that monarchies without popular elections are democracies, since the people have given sovereignty to the monarch (a consent that the people demonstrate when they refrain from revolution). Broad essentializing definitions of *democracy* have apologized for dictatorships, oligarchies, and monarchies alike.

To refute an essentializing definition, you must show that the definition either excludes something the audience would rather include in the category or admits something they would rather exclude from the category. Let's illustrate with an example that reflects a somewhat recent event: Imagine that the U.S. federal government has attempted to seize the cattle belonging to a rancher who let his herd graze on public lands without paying for the privilege. Your friend defines this as "government overreach." To refute that definition, you will have to point out that your friend's definition either admits things he would rather not define as "government overreach" or excludes things he would prefer to define as "government overreach":

- "If seizing cattle because someone owes the government leasing fees for the privilege of using federal land is an example of 'government overreach,' then so is the IRS's seizing assets or garnishing wages from people who refuse to pay their taxes."
- "If government overreach pertains only to cases that involve armed federal officers, then laws requiring affirmative action, healthcare reform, and environmental regulation are not 'government overreach' until citizens are forced to hire minorities, buy health insurance, or drive fuel-efficient cars at gunpoint."

Both of these imagined refutations claim that the following definitions essentialize the notion of "government overreach": (1) any effort to confiscate private property as a penalty for refusing payment to the federal government; (2) any law enforced by armed officers. Our refutations aim to convince the audience that the first definition includes too many things and the second excludes too many.

Reification

Reification is another flawed version of the argument at the topic of definition. A *reified* definition mistakenly assumes that words correspond to the audience's experience of real things. The word itself, *reification*, derives from the Latin word for "thing": res. Literally, *reification* means, "thingification." Consider a commonly reified term: "intelligence quotient" (IQ). We typically assume that a person's IQ is a thing that exists in the mind. Just as you measure the length of your foot, you measure the size of your IQ. Yet psychologists have argued for decades over whether anything like IQ really exists. Many allege that IQ is simply a made-up definition, a score earned on a test, correlating to no specific innate ability or quality. Like "spiritual energy," they say that "IQ" is a reified term with no relation to actual things in the world. Likewise, biologists occasionally argue about whether definitions of species are reifications with no correspondence to the real animals in the world. Earlier, when discussing the definition of *mammal*, we admitted that the duck-billed platypus calls this definition into question. So does the spiny anteater. Maybe there are no *mammals* per se, just animals on an evolutionary spectrum.

To refute a reified definition, you should point out that the speaker's preferred words have no relation to what people actually experience every day. This refutation depends upon your audience's specific experiences. Once the audience sees that the definition does not represent anything in their lived experiences, they will begin to question the argument.

Equivocation

Equivocation is a third flawed argument at the topic of definition. Equivocation happens when a speaker uses a definition in two completely different ways to mean two completely different things. For example, someone might argue that the right to free speech includes both the ability to express ideas without fear of legal punishment and the right to say anything in a public setting: "I have a right to free speech. The U.S. government can't punish me for criticizing the president. My neighbor can't sue me for saying I don't like him. And you can't stop me from speaking my mind at this PTA meeting." Such an argument suggests that *right* means two things: (1) a person's ability to do something without fear of legal retribution, and (2) a person's freedom to do something whenever she wants. The best way to refute an equivocating argument is to point out the different meanings assigned to the same word. To our imaginary equivocator, for instance, you could say, "You're talking about two things: rights and privileges. You have a right to speak your mind. No one will sue you or put you in jail for criticizing the school board's decision. But you don't have the privilege of interrupting this PTA meeting."

Slippery Slope

A slippery slope argument is a flawed inference that happens at the topic of causation. The speaker asserts that one action will start things down on a *slippery slope* that leads to all sorts of terrible effects. In an earlier chapter, we mentioned the claim that legalizing gay marriage will lead to legalizing polygamy. An audience might be persuaded to oppose gay marriage because it will lead to legalized polygamy, but this same audience might not be convinced to oppose gay marriage because it will lead to legalized bestiality. The difference between a persuasive and a flawed argument about causation is determined by the audience's willingness to believe that the effects are likely. Here's another example to illustrate: During the recent financial crisis, many people argued that the U.S. government had to rescue failing banks and insurance firms, for if such a rescue didn't happen, then financial and economic depression would result. Many people did not believe that such a result was likely. They pointed to investment firms that were allowed to fail—such as Bear Stearns and Lehmann Brothers—claiming that the predicted financial collapse did not follow from these firms' collapse. In sum, these people refused to believe that there was a slippery slope from failed investment firms to global financial crisis. But enough people did think that global financial collapse could result from a series of bank failures, so the U.S. government bailed out the banks.

To refute a slippery-slope argument, you must show your audience that the predicted results will not likely happen. If a giant pipeline is built to move oil from Canadian wells to U.S. refineries, why won't drilling destroy Canada's boreal forest? If tenure is abolished, why won't talented young people refuse to become teachers?

Post Hoc Ergo Propter Hoc

Post hoc ergo propter hoc is Latin for "after this, and therefore as a result of this." It refers to another flawed argument at the topic of causation. We tend to assume, quite reasonably, that sequence is a sign of causation. If one thing consistently follows another thing, then we assume that the two are causally related. But often that assumption is simply wrong-headed. Many Democrats said that the economic boom that came after Bill Clinton became president was a result of Clinton's presidency. And these same Democrats claimed that the recession that followed George W. Bush's election was a result of Bush's presidency. A skeptical audience might say that the president's actions have little direct effect on economic growth during the first few years in office. For this skeptical audience, saying that an election in 2001 caused an economic recession in 2002 is a classic example of *post hoc ergo propter hoc* argumentation.

Whether or not an audience will accept an argument at the topic of causation depends on that audience's presuppositions and the evidence that they require. If they're already willing to associate good economic performance with Democratic leadership, then they may take the sequence of events (first a Democrat wins the presidency, and then the economy gets better) as proof of causation. But if they're skeptical of that connection, then they will want more evidence. To refute a *post hoc ergo propter hoc* argument, you can point out that more evidence is needed to prove causation. Sequence, in this case, is not enough to prove causation.

Rebuttal

Our discussion of the different flawed arguments and the ways to refute them comes back to the same point over and over again: The quality of an argument depends on how an audience receives it. If beauty is in the eye of the beholder, then reason is in the ear of the listener. The same argument at the topic of causation will seem perfectly sound to some people and *post hoc ergo propter hoc* to others. The same definition will seem like an equivocation to some audience members and a sensible claim to others. Your job is to

Brief Exercise: Argue against yourself to improve your work. Return to the arguments that you invented to support your claims, and pretend that you're writing as someone who opposes your viewpoint. If you've written the short writing assignment at the end of Chapter 8, simply open that file to revisit the reasons you invented. After reading each reason, try to refute it. If you invented an argument at the topic of definition, explain why it's really an instance of reification or equivocation. If you invented an argument at the topic of causation, explain why it's really a slippery-slope argument. After you've thoroughly refuted yourself, revise your initial arguments so that an opponent will not be able to refute them so easily.

show the audience why they should question your opponent's claims. Simply saying, "that's reification" won't convince anyone to reject an argument. But explaining to your audience why a definition does not match their specific lived experience will lead them to question your opponent's viewpoint. Ultimately, that's all refutation can do. It can lead your audience to question arguments that they might otherwise have believed. To complete the effort, you need to rebut your opponent's arguments. After you've explained why your opponent's position is flawed, you should reiterate what your position is and why it's right.

Rebuttal is the return to argumentative offense. You've conceded that some of your opponent's ideas are reasonable. You've shown, where you could, that these reasonable ideas should support your principal claim. You've also shown that some of your opponent's arguments are flawed. Your audience, after these concessions and refutations, trusts you and doubts your opponent. Now, remind your audience of your viewpoint, and give additional reasons to convince them. This combination of concession, refutation, and rebuttal can be very effective. You don't have to do all three, and you don't have to do them in the order we prescribe. But mixing concession, refutation, and rebuttal into a long argument will make for a convincing claim.

Brief Exercise: Letters to the editor in newspapers and comments attached to online articles offer audience members an opportunity to practice concession, refutation, and rebuttal. Pick an article that you find interesting or convincing, something relevant to the controversy you've chosen to research this semester. Read the letters to the editor in response to this article. Letters to the editor typically get printed 3–7 days after the article appears. If the argument has been published online, read the comments people have posted. (If it's only been published online, then just read the comments.) Try to classify each sentence in these letters and/or comments as an instance of *concession*, *refutation*, or *rebuttal*. What general conclusions can you draw about how people in this venue typically oppose one another? Do they tend to go straight for rebuttal? Do they spend most of their time refuting? Do they ever concede? Evaluate the typical manner of opposing a viewpoint. Do you think more concession, refutation, or rebuttal would make these letters/comments more persuasive?

CHAPTER 10 | Arranging an Argument

If you were an ancient Greek or Roman lawyer-in-training, your instructor would first teach you to invent as many arguments and counterarguments as you could. You would select the best reasons to support your claims. Then you would move to the next step, arrangement. After you learned what you could say and after choosing the best reasons to support your case, you would be ready to put things in the most persuasive order. This final chapter, in a similar fashion, teaches you to arrange the arguments you learned to invent while reading Chapters 8 and 9.

Types of Arrangement

Unlike invention, arrangement is often approached formulaically. Writers follow arrangement templates, often called "boilerplates." They put the right parts in the right places. In the social sciences, for example, articles presenting new research tend to be arranged into four sections: (1) an explanation of the question or hypothesis that the researcher wants to answer; (2) a description of the methods that the researcher will use to answer this question; (3) a description of the data collected while applying this method; (4) an analysis of the data, featuring conclusions. Seen this way, writing a research article for an academic journal in the social sciences seems a bit like painting by numbers. If you follow the steps, you'll write a good essay.

Such boilerplates are useful. We encourage you to learn them. But we also point out that boilerplates, by themselves, ignore the most important factor in arrangement—the audience. A boilerplate makes it seem like a good arrangement always follows a specific form. But the truth is that an effective arrangement presents information to a specific audience. Sometimes the boilerplate can guide the writer to meet the audience's needs. But having all the parts arranged according to the boilerplate is less important than meeting the audience's expectations. Social scientists expect researchers to ask new questions, to contribute new information, and to build on past research. The boilerplate that we describe above accomplishes these tasks. So social scientists appreciate articles that follow this template. Once an audience has learned a boilerplate, the arrangement shapes their expectations. Once upon a time, when the social sciences were new disciplines, there were many people with the same expectations but no boilerplates to guide their writing. As they wrote to meet one another's expectations, they developed a template, which they all began to follow. Now students in the social sciences learn the boilerplate, and from the boilerplate, they learn to expect certain things from social-science writing.

Our main point is that good arrangement suits the audience's expectations. Often, a boilerplate will guide you to a good arrangement, but you should keep in mind that a boilerplate is a rough guide to what a specific audience will likely expect. If the audience's expectations differ from what is typical, the speaker must deviate from the boilerplate. Allow us to illustrate with two more examples of commonly used boilerplates.

The Specific-General Pyramid

The specific-general pyramid guides many information articles found in news venues. Journalism students learn this boilerplate because it meets the expectations of newspaper audiences. An article following this arrangement strategy will begin by mentioning specific information about a recent event. The first paragraph (or two) will offer details about a recent election, a murder, or a city council meeting. Subsequent paragraphs gradually introduce more background information to explain the specific event. A regular newspaper reader who has followed an election will not want to read all the background information—which candidate ran for which office under which party's umbrella—because she will already know this information. She just wants to know the election results. So she reads the first few paragraphs and stops. On the other hand, a different reader who hasn't been following a story will want all the background information. When he reads the first few paragraphs of an article about a bond election to fund road construction, he might realize that he should learn more, so he reads the whole article.

Our example illustrates that the specific-general pyramid addresses the needs of two audiences: those who already know about a story and those who don't know but want to learn. A third audience is possible—those who don't know and don't yet care. For them, the savvy journalist will have to deviate from the specific-general boilerplate. Her article might open with a story about a particular person to show the audience why they should care. If she can grab the audience's interest by telling them a moving story about someone who suffers from Parkinson's disease, then she can get them to read an article about breakthroughs in genetic research. Throughout the article, this same journalist might occasionally say more about this person to keep the audience interested. The audience's concern for an individual patient keeps them interested in the details of medical science. And to appeal to that concern, the speaker must deviate from the specific-general pyramid.

The Five-Paragraph Essay

Without a doubt, you learned to write a five-paragraph essay in your middle or high school English classes. The all-too-familiar arrangement is: (1) an introductory paragraph that discusses a broad topic an d concludes with a thesis statement; (2) three body paragraphs, each beginning with a topic sentence and each supporting the introductory paragraph's thesis statement; (3) a concluding paragraph that restates the thesis statement. The five-paragraph essay is the height of formulaic writing. After mastering this arrangement scheme, many students are disappointed to learn that it does not satisfy all audiences. The five-paragraph essay, nonetheless, does meet the expectations of writing teachers, especially those teaching inexperienced writers. This arrangement showcases the basic skills that will help students even after they've finished the last concluding paragraph of the last five-paragraph essay that they will write in their senior year of high school. The five-paragraph essay shows the teacher that a student can briefly state an argument. This arrangement also shows that the student can present several bits of evidence to support that argument. Finally, a well-written five-paragraph essay shows that the student can manage transitions from one paragraph to the next. In short, the five-paragraph essay shows the writing teacher that the student has learned important writing skills. And that's what writing teachers expect to see in student work.

The five-paragraph essay is also useful for another audience—people who grade the exam portion of the SAT. But this audience has somewhat different expectations, so following the same five-paragraph essay boilerplate may get you into trouble. To begin with, graders do not have the time or the energy to read your essay carefully. They typically grade a stack of essays all at one time, dedicating seven or maybe ten minutes to each. Additionally, they are looking for specific evidence rather than reasons. While the College Board (the organization that makes and grades the SAT) says that a good essay will include "clearly appropriate examples, reasons, and other evidence to support its position," most guides to the SAT emphasize that writers should focus on examples because that is the first thing listed by the College Board and because examples are easy for a grader to find. So you must modify the five-paragraph essay boilerplate to meet this new audience's expectations. You must write a brief introductory paragraph that states its thesis as quickly and as clearly as possible. You must write a few (maybe three, maybe more, or maybe fewer) paragraphs, each featuring at least one example and each introduced by a clear transition. (The College Board also mentions that a good SAT essay will be "well organized and clearly focused, demonstrating clear coherence and smooth progression of ideas.")

Your arrangement must highlight the transitions and the examples to make sure a tired grader doesn't overlook them if he is reading his 25th essay late one Tuesday afternoon.

Experienced writers have learned many boilerplates, so they can write for many different audiences. And you should do the same. But as you learn these arrangement strategies, keep in mind that you're really learning strategies for dealing with various audiences' expectations.

> **Brief Exercise:** The College Board has published descriptions of SAT essays here: http://professionals.collegeboard. com/testing/sat-reasoning/scores/ essay/guide. After reading these descriptions, describe the College Board. What does this audience—SAT essay graders—expect? What kind of boilerplate would you develop to meet this audience's expectations?

Classical Template

Your third major assignment in RHE 306 is a persuasive essay. Since audiences come to persuasive essays with particular expectations, you can anticipate those expectations and arrange accordingly. The persuasive argument and the audience expecting to be persuaded are nothing new, so there is an antique boilerplate that you may find useful. This is the classical template, a flexible arrangement strategy that was taught—in one way or another—by ancient Greeks and Romans and that guides—in one form or another—contemporary arguments. As we present it, the classical template has six major components: exordium, narration, partition, argument, refutation, and peroration. Each part attempts to meet and then shape the audience's expectations. Since audiences vary, each part of the classical template can do a range of things. An exordium, for example, does not always have to introduce the topic or interest the audience. And a persuasive essay does not have to include an exordium. As Aristotle once explained, a persuasive argument needs only two parts: a claim and a reason to believe that claim. Such a simple, two-part arrangement would only meet the expectations of audiences who are informed, enthusiastic, and ready to fairly consider your ideas. Since this ideal audience rarely exists, you need a more versatile boilerplate, one you can adapt to a range of audiences. The classical template exhibits such versatility.

Exordium

You've heard the term "introduction" before. Introductions typically accomplish a few things. An introduction may tell the audience the general topic that the argument will cover. It may give background information that the audience needs to know. It may give the audience a reason to care about the controversy. An introduction may also clarify any confusion that the audience might have. And it will probably state the argument's principal claim or thesis. The classical template's exordium attempts many of the tasks assigned to contemporary introductions. But the classical exordium does a lot less and a little more than the contemporary introduction.

An exordium must grab the audience's attention, sparking their interes t and earning their trust. If your audience comes ready to hear the argument, then you don't need much of an exordium. If they are interested in the topic, then you don't have to raise their interest. If they're excited about the controversy, then you don't have to show them why they should care. Finally, if they're sympathetic to your cause and if they are confident in you as the speaker, then you don't have to win their approval.

However, an exordium written to an uninterested audience *must* grab their attention. This is usually accomplished by presenting a reason to feel excited or concerned about the topic. The typical exordium to a disinterested audience opens with a vivid description: If you wanted to convince your audience to care about women's equality in other countries, you could open with an example of a girl who has been denied an education by religious fundamentalists in Pakistan. If you want to convince your audience that they should care about tax breaks that encourage local businesses in small-town Texas, you could describe Fredericksburg's flourishing downtown. An exordium written to a suspicious audience must give them a reason to trust you. Introduce yourself. Explain your credentials. Show the audience that you bear them goodwill.

As our description suggests, the exordium offers a brief space at the beginning of your argument, a place where you can give your audience reasons to feel excited or concerned about the subject. Furthermore, the exordium is an opportunity to give the audience a reason to trust you as a speaker. The audience may already feel interested, and they may already have confidence in you. For such an audience, the exordium simply needs to start the argument. Such an exordium may be as brief as, "Let's talk about welfare reform."

Narration

The narration gives the audience the background information they will need in order to understand the argument that follows. The narration does not have to immediately follow the exordium. And bits of narration can be spread around the entire composition. You may find it more effective to insert narration at various points in the argument, giving your audience new background information as you introduce new ideas.

Although no strategy applies to every audience, you can begin to plan the narration by considering two factors: the audience's feeling toward the subject and the audience's knowledge about the subject. An audience that feels averse to a subject may require a long narration to coax them toward a different disposition. The narration, in this case, would be entirely at the beginning of the argument. If, for example, you were arguing against the use of medical marijuana before an audience who supported complete legalization, then you might begin your argument with an extended narration of the drug's history. Though these people may already know the history of marijuana—the laws and the effects relating to the drug—your narration can give them reasons to feel worried by telling a history that emphasizes the drug's negative side, its connection to crime and its dubious medical value. Along the way, your extended narration will give them a reason to trust you as an authority on the subject.

On the other hand, an audience that is ignorant of the subject will need a narration that brings them up to speed, defining key terms, detailing important events, and introducing major players. Such a narration may partly appear at the argument's beginning. To introduce an ignorant audience to the subject, you can give them basic information about the controversy in the first few paragraphs. Then, as your argument develops, you can insert moments of narration to provide background information as it's needed. If quickly and deftly inserted, such narrative moments can inform an ignorant audience without disrupting the flow of the argument. These are narrative *digressions*: passages that turn away from the principal argument to accomplish some necessary but secondary task.

As we've emphasized, the narration can give the audience reasons to feel something about your subject; it can give them a reason to trust you as a speaker; and it can provide the audience with the background information they need to understand the argument. While the narration is not an opportune moment to present reasons to believe, it can set up later appeals by providing crucial bits of evidence that you can recall later in the essay. And, of course, a narration need not do any of this. If the audience is informed, sympathetic, and trusting, then you can skip the narration altogether.

Partition

Two kinds of sentences that you've no doubt learned about elsewhere are very basic forms of a partition: thesis statements and topic sentences. A thesis statement is a very brief partition at the end of an introduction. A topic sentence is an even briefer partition at the beginning of a paragraph. In a long argument, the partition prepares the audience by forecasting the principal claim and the manner of argument. A partition announces to the audience, "Hear ye! Hear ye! This is what I will say, and this is how I will say it!" Detailed partitions are especially appropriate when writing to an easily confused audience. If the argument is complicated, any audience will have trouble following it. If the audience is particularly inexperienced, they will have trouble following any argument. In either case, it's a good idea to tell them what's coming down the pike.

Partitions, though very functional, can be burdensome, and they're rarely elegant. It's hard to sound mellifluous or poetic when saying something like this:

> In this argument, I will give three reasons and substantial evidence to support my claim that carbon offsets are an ineffective way to address global climate change. First, I will define carbon offsets as a marketing gimmick, often called "greenwashing." Then I will show why those selling carbon offsets should enrage rather than placate anyone who considers herself an environmentalist. Finally, using examples of two companies that sell carbon offsets for air travel, I will demonstrate that these programs do not achieve their promised effects.

Such a partition, though clear, is also dull. If the audience can follow the argument without a detailed partition, you should jump into the argument. If the audience needs a detailed partition but you don't want to bore them at the outset, then you can opt for brief partitions inserted at key moments. At the beginning of each major section, using a transition statement, you can remind your audience of the previous reason and introduce the next one:

> Having seen that most carbon offsets are nothing more than "greenwashing," you should understand why no environmentalist should feel good about them. In fact, we should feel angry that companies would sell them at all.

Of course, it's possible that your audience will have no trouble following your argument, so they will not need any partition. Furthermore, including a partition risks turning away a hostile audience, for people often shut their ears once they hear something they don't like. Speakers addressing hostile audiences might therefore risk a confusing presentation just to make sure that the audience won't tune them out.

Argument

The argument is, as the name implies, the meat of any persuasive essay. After preparing the audience, narrating the background, and forecasting the arrangement, finally the speaker presents her reasons. A couple pieces of standard advice can help you think about this section of your essay:

- *Though the argument is the most important part of your essay, it may not be the longest segment of your essay.* As we suggest above, the first three parts in the classical template may take a lot of space. If you're writing to a hostile audience that is ignorant on the subject, you will have to win their trust and provide copious background information. The exordium and the narration may take up half of the entire essay. If you're writing to a sympathetic but disinterested and easily confused audience, you will have to get them excited and prepare them for a complex argument. The exordium and partition may take up a third of your essay. The basic lesson is that sometimes it takes more work to prepare an audience than it takes to convince them.
- *The argument itself must be arranged.* You will likely have several reasons and a decent amount of evidence to present. You want to sequence this information together effectively. One strategy is to present your reasons and your evidence so that they reinforce one another. If, for instance, an image will elicit certain emotions only after you've earned the audience's trust, then you should begin by giving your audience reasons to trust you. Another strategy is to arrange your reasons in an ascending pattern from the least persuasive to the most persuasive. This way, your audience's commitment will steadily increase. And a third strategy is to place your weakest reason between your strongest reasons: Open with a convincing reason; follow with a less convincing reason; and conclude with the most convincing reason. Your audience will remember the reasons that you present first and last; they will forget the stuff in the middle.

Refutation

Chapter 9 offers strategies for refuting an opponent's arguments so you can counterargue. The question now is, when to counterargue? In the classical template, refutation comes after the argument. You've made your case. Now show your audience why the opposition's viewpoint is flawed. This arrangement—first argument, then refutation—assumes that the audience is ready to hear the argument. And this arrangement further assumes that, after hearing the argument, the audience will be mostly convinced; all that remains is to push the opposition aside. But sometimes an audience is so committed to the opposing viewpoint that they will not consider an argument unless they first hear a refutation (or some mixture of refutation, concession, and rebuttal). In this case, you should lead with the refutation. In fact, when addressing an especially hostile audience, speakers often choose to spend most of their time refuting the opposition, inserting the argument at opportune moments. For these reasons and many others, we encourage you to think of the refutation as a part of your arrangement that can move around as needed. Like narration, refutation can occur just about anywhere. Like partition, refutation should appear where it is best suited to the audience's expectations.

Peroration

The peroration is the last thing your audience will read. Contemporary conclusions typically repeat the argument's principal claim. In the five-paragraph essay, for example, the introduction and the conclusion both feature the thesis statement. If you're writing to an audience that has trouble following the argument, then you should restate your principal claim in the peroration. Remind them of what you've said. But if you're writing to an audience that will easily remember your principal claim, then you can do other things in your peroration. Two options immediately present themselves:

- *You can give the audience reasons to feel.* Perorations are often emotional because the speaker must inspire the audience to act or because the speaker wants to make the audience strongly commit to a belief.
- *You can give the audience reasons to believe something new.* If the audience is already sufficiently convinced of your principal claim, then you can extend it by suggesting further implications—other beliefs that follow from your argument.

Like the exordium, the peroration is an optional part of the classical template. If you've made your case well enough, if it's inappropriate to raise emotions, and if it's impossible to prove any new claims, then you can simply end the essay minimally, without a peroration.

Having discussed the classical template, we leave the final decisions about arrangement to you, the speaker.

Brief Exercise: Now that you know the six parts of the classical template, analyze the arrangement chosen by a fellow student writer. On your RHE 306 Canvas site is a student-authored persuasive essay. Read through it. Next to each paragraph (or each sentence), describe that part of the essay, using the classical template's vocabulary. Are the first few sentences (or the entire first paragraph) an exordium? Does the second paragraph offer both a narration and partition? Where is the refutation? After describing the arrangement, evaluate it. Do you think the argument could be more persuasively arranged? How?

Further Discussion: When you are considering the best manner of arrangement for your argument, the classical template will serve in most rhetorical situations; however, there are instances in which audiences may not initially trust you enough to listen to anything you have to say. If the audience is particularly hostile or suspicious, a better approach can be to reverse the classical template and compose what is called a Rogerian argument. This type of argumentation derives from the client-centered philosophy of American psychologist Carl Rogers, who felt that communication requires an atmosphere of trust. There are several strategies for doing so. The following arrangement template distills those strategies into a Rogerian boilerplate:

1. Introduce your argument with a neutral, objective restatement of the opposition's position. Don't even hint at your own position. The whole point is to demonstrate that you understand the audience's point of view and can articulate it in a way that they will accept.

2. Begin each body paragraph by targeting a shared value. For example, if you are writing an argument about the need for more gun control and you are addressing the argument to an audience of NRA members, you might begin one of your body paragraphs by writing something like this: "As concerned citizens, we all believe in protecting our children against those who would do them harm." Although the ways in which you and an audience of NRA members think children should be protected may differ, you both value your children's safety. It is important that you do not begin by arguing your own position. Concede that your audience is right in many ways, and point out some of the problems associated with using guns to protect children. You might, for example, open with a narrative about how a parent successfully used a gun to protect his family from an intruder and then offer some equally compelling statistical evidence that suggests children are more likely to suffer harm when their parents keep guns at home. For many, gun control is a black-and-white issue; Rogerian argumentation attempts to make polarizing issues like gun control more complex.

3. Finally, in your conclusion, state your principal claim(s). By this time, your audience should trust you enough to listen to what you have to say. And because you have been fair and neutral in your treatment of the issue, they will have good reasons to question their deeply held beliefs and consider your point of view.